MW01241106

Transparency

Insights Into the Creative Process

Jerrell Golden, Sr.

This is a work of creative nonfiction. This book or parts thereof may not be duplicated in any form, stored in a recovery system, or transmitted in any form by any means – electronic, mechanical, photocopy, recording, or otherwise – without permission from the publisher, except as provided by the United States of America copyright law.

Copyright © 2022 by Jerrell Golden, Sr.

All rights reserved. No part of this book may be reproduced or used in any manner without written permission of the copyright owner except for the use of quotations in a book review.

Unless otherwise noted, all Scripture quotations are from the New Living Translation Version of the Bible. Used by permission.

First paperback edition September 2022.

Golden Touch Creations products are available at special quantity discounts for bulk purchase for sales promotions, fundraising, and educational needs.

Book designs by Golden Touch Creations

International Standard Book Number: 979-8-218-08414-1

Printed in the United States of America

Published by Golden Touch Creations

jerrell-golden.online

Dedication

This book is dedicated to my beautiful mother, Tresa Ann Golden.

You've been an inspiration to me in more ways than I can count, and I thank God for your place in my heart.

I love you, ma!

Table of Contents

Introduction

Nakedness.

When I think of nakedness, a few words come to mind, such as: bare, stripped, exposed, and vulnerable.

However, when I look at nakedness from a biblical standpoint, I envision one that's unashamed, free, and unconfined.

When God initially created Adam and Eve, they were naked, both physically and spiritually.

Physically, meaning that they were without clothing. They knew no shame, nor had any sense of embarrassment, due to the fact that they knew they were made in the image of a perfect and righteous God.

Their spiritual nakedness meant that they had nothing to hide from God.

The intimacy of their relationship with God was without any restrictions or distractions.

They were open with Him at all times, and He honored their openness by walking with them in the cool of the day.

Once sin was introduced into humanity, we began to see Adam and Eve operate in a way that God did not like.

To be brief, in **Genesis Chapter 2, verses 16 and 17,** God made it clear to Adam that he could freely eat from any tree in the garden, except for the tree of the knowledge of good and evil.

At that time Eve had not yet been created; in other words, she had not received that instruction.

The instruction was given to Adam, who was to pass the word of God on to his wife after she was formed.

After the creation of Eve, it is not written in God's word that Adam relayed that information to his wife, which could easily be seen as the root of why she was so easily manipulated by satan.

Her husband did not share with her the word of God.

The intimacy God wants to share with us is predicated on how naked we are willing to be with Him.

While being vulnerable and open may sound like signs of weakness to some, God infuses those qualities with His Holy Spirit, allowing both to then be areas where we are able to minister to others.

As I look back over my life prior to Christ, I see how confused I was. I see how tied down and burdened I was with the desire for acceptance and the approval of my peers in the communities that I was a part of.

I was after the pursuit of pleasure and all that came along with it, having once "received it."

The same way Adam and Eve began to clothe themselves due to their poor choices, I spent years distancing myself from God, thinking that I could figure this thing called life out on my own.

The amazing thing about it all is that regardless of how many layers I threw on, I later found out that God was still willing to accept and love me through all of my mess.

Appreciating His love for me is what led me to give my life to Him, transforming my lifestyle to one that's pleasing to Him.

As you continue to read on, you will obtain a vivid look at my transition from being a man, to a man of God [as based on my album, *Transparency*].

Each chapter will represent my state of mind at that particular time of the creative process.

I am a firm believer that content without a message is a dangerous narrative; one that can indeed become toxic to whomever is on the receiving end.

So, in each chapter I will thoroughly explain why I wrote the things that I did, allowing you to fully grasp the vision that was within me at that time.

I believe explaining it this way will allow you to feel what I felt during each moment.

I'd now like to welcome you to "Transparency".

Philippians Chapter 3, verses 12 through 16

"Not that I have already obtained it, this goal of being Christ-like or have been made perfect but I actively press on so that I may take hold of that perfection for which Christ Jesus took hold of me and made me His own. Brothers and sisters, I do not consider that I have made it my own yet, but one thing I do, forgetting what lies behind and reaching forward to what lies ahead. I press on to win the goal, that heavenly prize of the upward call of God in Christ Jesus."

Transparency

*For your listening pleasure: scan the QR Code at the top of each chapter, and you can play each song as you progress along.

Chapter 1: "Transparency"

(Intro)
There comes a point in time
when you just gotta be real with yourself.

Can't keep lookin in the mirror expecting
to see something that you're not.

That joint might feel good for a lil
while....and everybody's a "little while" is
different, you feel me.....

Some peoples a "lil while" may be a month
or....
For some people it might be 2 or 3 years
but....

If I'm being honest, my lil while was
10years....
10 years!!!
I was lost....
I just wanna talk about it for little bit

(Verse)
Same two step, but a different beat
See I begin every day with faith my ends
meet
The Alpha and, the Omega's who I then
seek
First that's why His Spirit's what you're
hearing when my pen leak
I used to think I had it figured out
a lil pip-squeak
Drowning in my sin had me tippy-toeing
six feet
Till God showed me that it's He who opens
doors so
Now to level up I twist the handle like a six
speed
I used to beef with my momma after stiff
drinks
Outside her house around the corner, I
would spliff trees
Mad cologne trying to hide the loud scent
Cuz money talks and I ain't have to ask
Chris Tucker or Charlie Sheen
Momma she ain't stupid she knew game
seen my eyes low

9

While I was Visining, she praying with her
eyes closed
My lil bro was only three, both our fathers
MIA
Ironically...I was daddy in his eyes tho
But I was slow to comprehend that I was
blind bro

The prodigal son, corrupted in the mind yo
That teenage Rock naw I ain't got no time
for
Church or Jesus naw you can keep that cuz
my mind on them thighs on
Shorty over there....

Sippin 40s of that O.E. cuz homie told me
the OGs
use to buck it so you know me
My nose clean but I blow tree, thinkin I'm
lowkey
At Wal Mart smoking in public like folks
don't know me
Or my family
Mom's getting hit up
People telling her how they seen me and I
was lit up
I got stories for days of the many ways
I done slipped up
But it all leads to His grace and the ways
He done picked up

*Youngin outta the hiccups now I'm
swallowing truth
Regurgitating the facts giving you the
good fruit
Cuz the body needs its nourishment
I've been given the juice
So when I concentrate
my squeeze is being put to good use
true!!!*

*It's all facts no printers
I'd rather trust Acts than pretenders
My sword is like an ax for the splinters
The map gave His life and His back
and took crack after crack for us sinners
And I callem the map
cuz He's the way, truth and life
The omnipresent prototype
the ultimate sacrifice
In retrospect
His mercy uncovered my eyes
So as I expound on my darkness
I pray you see His light*

"Transparency"

Being real with yourself first begins with knowing who you are.

In the part where I said, "You can't keep looking in the mirror expecting to see something that you're not," I was single-handedly basing that truth off of my younger self.

During my high school years, between the ages of 16 and 18, I genuinely struggled with my identity.

Not in the sense of being confused as to who I was in regard to my gender, but who I was as a person.

I was a walking question mark, adapting to whoever was around me, and taking on their personas to fit in.

I often mixed my desires to be accepted by my peers, with the HipHop culture that I was in love with. I was, as some would say, "lost in the sauce."

Back then, HipHop was the most influential thing in my life.

I also noticed how it played a huge role in the lives of my friends.

I wanted to have what the rappers had, so I could talk about what the rappers talked about.

I've always had a connection with being able to relate to something.

So as weird as this may sound, even if I was making the wrong decisions in being a follower, I somehow justified the wrongdoing in my mind because I could relate to the people I was following.

I knew that my mom did not like me smoking cigarettes, and she absolutely did not like knowing that I smoked weed.

Her overall rule was, "Not in my house! You take that mess somewhere else."

Ultimately, that led to me continuously breaking my curfew.

My dad was nowhere in the picture then, so it was just me, my little brother, and my mom.

I didn't know it then, but the more and more that I rebelled against my mom and her house-rules, I was putting a strain on being present in my little brother's life.

At that time, he was only 3 years old, and his father was not with him on a regular basis.

He looked at me as more of a father-figure, as opposed to a big brother.

Throughout all of the wrongs that I committed back then, it amazed me to hear about a God who not only knew me personally, but who was also ready and willing to forgive me.

I then fast forward to post-salvation; I speak of how I now aim to share my life's story alongside the gospel of Jesus Christ.

This is all done in an effort to restore hope in those who desire it.

I now understand that my life, absent from God's heart, will only lead to distractions and disaster.

It was only through God's forgiving heart (mercy), and His unearned love (grace), that I'm a free man who can now talk about all of this today.

In the next chapter, I peel back a couple more layers so you can get a better look at the person I used to be back in high school and after graduating.

To be honest, all I can do is shake my head when I think about the old me at times.

Chapter 2:
"Breathe"

(Verse 1)
I was told I better go and get it
won't nobody gonna give it to me
I was told to hold my position
won't nobody gonna get through me
I was in the middle
I was in the middle
ears open eyes looking clueless
All I knew is that I wanted music
all I knew is that I wanted music

Everybody wanna sell me drugs
cuz I rap about being high
Everybody talking bout the plug
never was I ever that guy
White tee down to my knees
fitted to the back call that fly
Du-rag untied with the strings

matching my slouch-socks (ahh)
Won't nothing you could ever tell me
mama tried, all we did was beef
At that time I was doing me
At that time I was in the streets

Lowkey wit my own crew
'09 living like '02
Young-minded
Young-minded
Immature
Marques Houston
I was in the passenger with the seat back
On Mbuzzy
getting chics
they'd MySpace me I'd tweet back
I had avenues
avenues
in Tappahannock where the streets at
But I'm Millers Tavern
I-Neck
on the back roads where my streets at look

Just let it breathe

(Verse 2)
30 on'em with the pen
sweet wit da flow need insulin ugh
God gave it to me
can't brag gotta give it back to Him
Abba

17

I remember when I had my mommas .380
Fronting on the block
tryna shoot a stop sign
wit a house right behind it crazy
bad aim....(bad aim)
great grace....(great grace)
Not one bullet hit they house on that day my
Lord
Could've been an involuntary
manslaughter charge easily
but you didn't let it happen
God what you see in me

I was stealing liquor gettin zoot
me and Killa Leta on the step
Freestyling looking at the stars
thinking like yo we the best
Way before Khaled ever said it
we said it
I won't forget it

Can't nobody ever tell me that I
wasn't confident enough to go and get it
(Nah)
but what was I getting
other than what you was giving
Not a thing
now I see it so clearly

Yahweh I'm indebted
born sinner

perfection is nowhere in my mirror
but by His grace
when you hit play
you get a different picture
Amen...
Now just...... Let it breathe

In 2002, I was in the 10th grade.

It was then that I first stepped foot into a studio.

It was also the first time that I heard myself on a recording.

Up until that point, I had only been freestyling with friends at school and the surrounding areas where I lived.

I knew I had skill, and based on the feedback from those who heard me, they knew it too.

HipHop taught me to be a "go-getter," and to stand my ground regardless of adversity or circumstances.

I followed that motto and incorporated that mindset into my craft.

I knew that the popular things to talk about were drugs, girls, sex, getting money, and violence; so, I followed suit.

In doing so, I piqued the interest of local drug dealers who then saw me as a potential customer.

Nevertheless, my lyrical content, as well as my look, were intentional because I wanted to reach the same people that HipHop reached.

During my misguided chase for recognition and acceptance, I can recall spending countless nights outside with my friends where I lived.

We'd be posted up at the stop sign beside the cedar tree... [If you know, you know!]

One night, I took my mom's .380 handgun out there with me and attempted to shoot the stop sign.

I believe it let off about 5 shots; none of them hit the sign.

It didn't dawn on me until years later that there had always been a family living in the house right behind that same stop sign.

It's moments like that where I'm left in awe of how much God cares about me.

Not only did He protect that family and their home, but He also protected me from the consequences that I inevitably would've faced if any of those bullets had hit that house.

Looking at God's grace after the fact should be a tool used to strengthen your faith in Him as you progress forward.

When I was getting drunk off of stolen liquor, I knew that my heart's desires had nothing to do with God, nor His will for my life.

I spent months in jail, nights sleeping outside, days walking the streets, and years manipulating people into getting the things that I wanted, all to have Christ Jesus still reveal Himself to me.

Now that I've received this new life in Christ, my mission is to go and tell everybody just how good God truly is.

Chapter 3: "Gotta"

(Intro)

I gotta go....I gotta get it....
I gotta go....I gotta get it....
I gotta go....I gotta get it....
I gotta go....I gotta get it....
I gotta go....I gotta get it....
I gotta go....I gotta get it....
I gotta go....I gotta get it....
I gotta go....I gotta get it....
I gotta go....I gotta get it....

I got a wife.... I got my children....
I got my faith....I gotta live it....
I got that juice...I gotta give it
ABBA done put me in I gotta vision
Started me on my way I gotta finish

*Share what I've been through bruh I gotta
witness
Do you know what I mean, do I got a
witness.....whew*

(Verse 1)
*I was living foul like roughing the kicker
throwing up E-Town wit a cup full of liquor
blunt smelling loud got thump in the Swisher
Hard to keep my feet down
I was up in the middle of confusion
Thought I was winning but bruh I was losing
Momma praying so much her knees was
bruisin
I was out here in these streets looking foolish
God got up in the middle said
Hold up boy pause that
You think you grown
you better know where the boss at
I've got stripes on my back you caused that
The way you living you really need to get off
that*

*He said follow me then you will see
I said ok look that's what I'm doing
putting God over all I'm not changing a thing
Matthew 6:33 homie I'm wit it look*

(Hook)
*I gotta go....I gotta get it....
I got a wife.... I got my children....*

I got my faith....I gotta live it....
I got that juice...I gotta give it
ABBA done put me in I gotta vision
Started me on my way I gotta finish
*Share what I've been through bruh I gotta
witness*
*Do you know what I mean, do I got a witness
look*
I gotta go....I gotta get it....(repeat 16xs)
(Verse 2)
One time I took a bunch of pills
trying to kill me
but I ain't die
another time I thought of suicide
but I thank God, that I didn't try
I just cried on God's shoulder
I was in a sunken place
felt like a waste of space
but then He came and told me move over
He took all my pain away
I'm so amazed at grace

*I hope that you know that He knows you
personally and know that that never will
change*
whatever you're facing He can fix it
I promise I put that on everything
Iron sharpens Iron
Ima need you to pick me up when I am low
We are the church
the body of Christ in these streets

24

we gotta go
do that
Level up.......true that.....
God's bloodshed was proof that
We done been forgiven for living so clueless
And it ain't all about money homie where you
at

So don't be lost out here trying to boss out
here
cuz the real boss out here is where the Truth's
at
you out here lovin on death
yo where they do that
......my Father...
Broke the mold you know there's no other
Toe to toe beat death like no problem
Jehovah Jireh, my provider
yuuuh...

Bruh...
I was livin just like you
and I still have my moments....
....I ain't perfect I know this....
but I know that I've gotta stay focused bruh

(Hook)
I gotta go....I gotta get it....
I got a wife.... I got my children....
I got my faith....I gotta live it....
I got that juice...I gotta give it

ABBA done put me in I gotta vision
Started me on my way I gotta finish
Share what I've been through bruh I gotta
witness
Do you know what I mean, do I got a witness
look
I gotta go....I gotta get it....(rpt 16xs)

There's something magical about being on fire for God.

Through all of the craziness I had experienced, when God revealed Himself to me, I began to literally see myself and my situations as I read His word.

I fast forwarded quite a few years.

In what I go on to share, I'd had a daughter, been in several relationships that ended on not-so-good terms, started dating a new girl which led to me being married, had a son, and received salvation.

"Gotta" exemplifies my hunger to tell people about this newfound relationship I had begun.

Not the relationship with my girlfriend, nor with my daughter or son.

My relationship with Jesus was far stronger than any of the others.

It was one of those feelings to where trying to explain it would often result in leaving me looking dumb in the face.

At that time, I couldn't fully break down the theology of the scriptures, or even expound upon the parables that Jesus taught.

Everything was merely based on my testimony, and that was what I used to tell people about His saving grace.

My life prior to salvation was pretty basic.

I literally did the same thing every day for about 10 years.

I was known in Tappahannock for my rapping abilities, and I made it my mission to represent home in everything that I did; hence me shouting out "E-Town" at the beginning of the verse.

"E-Town" is our way of shouting out Essex County, which is where the city of Tappahannock dwells.

My aim was to target the people who recognized me for my lifestyle back then, by telling them about who I had become.

I had gotten away from the area and was no longer a face that the locals saw every day. At that point, I knew I had their ear because they knew I was nice on the microphone.

I wanted their hearts, however, because I knew that's what God changed within me.

Speaking of my suicide attempts made me extremely uncomfortable at the time.

When I initially decided to put that information in a song, I knew people would judge me and take the news back to my mom.

The last thing I wanted to do was make her look back or stress herself out.

Nevertheless, it was stuff like that which allowed people to open up to me and tell their story; this, in turn, granted me the opportunity to share the gospel with them.

It was in realizing and believing that God knew me personally, that made the difference for me.

It opened me up to the idea of placing trust in what He had to say about me and my situations.

Once I started noticing changes for the better in my life, all I wanted was for others to experience their own personal joy as well.

Chapter 4: "Balance"

(Verse 1)

It's getting heavy, my shoulders bulging
Tho I'm not giving up this pressure's got my
dawgs barking gottem talkin....
Mass hatred.....satan's gawkin
The elephant inside the room I now can see is
heartless.....

Sin.......
Me another meme of Kaepernick down on one
knee
Send......
Me back to Black Wall Street where they
destroyed everything

Sin......

*Has been so evident but hidden within this
color thing*

*Send......
Me back to the garden where Adam
corrupted Heaven's dream.....*

*Being passive's the epitome of lacking action
Our insecurities look Moses-like
we need an Aaron*

*Initiate you learning you
that should not be an errand
This going over your head
simply shows your understanding
It's Black Lives Matter
every time somebody dies
But while we living
then it's throw yo sets up in the skies
The word woke has been twisted within us
givin us
A false sense of hope
when really for identity we cry*

*We pray for help and then take the credit
once God provides it
Full of ourselves
flesh eaters a sinners diet
But I'm here to tell you that
God's people are surely rising*

They out here preaching
that's why you see all these sinners dying

You can't live until you die, bruh get it right....
You can't live until you die bruh, get a life
I know some folks that when tested
they gotta get a light
When Abraham got tested he had to get a
knife
What are you sacrificing.....
Time, money, materials can't compare to a
life...
for which you fight

You gripping with all your might, you might
Slip and lose sight,
Of God's will
will you let, God enter or fight
The inner god in you in His image you were
given life from His eyes you were given sight
for your darkness you were given light
check yo balance

(Verse 2)
Appreciate your history
and don't become a Tobey
Was gon say Kunta but
Spur of the moment
went Ginobli
Flippin through scriptures
it's crazy to know them pages know me

That instruction manual to life
has never left me lonely
I'm seeing demons
slowly being sucked outta homies
They can't explain it
when I say it's Jesus
then they ignore me
I brush it off though inside
I'm having a hard time coping
because I know that they are so quick to say
they praying for me......
.....well who you praying to...........
God?
......Jesus is God
that's odd
fix your facade
You seen a picture of Jesus that's white
that can't be right
You're right
but Jesus is more than color bruh
He is life....

Jesus walking on water
you read it like yeah ok
I know that walking on water
we do it like everyday
Perspective is everything
we're not Jesus we're more like Peter
he took his eyes off of Jesus
and quickly started to sink
So trust me when I say

I could care less whatchu gotta say
Your ideologies
never will interfere with my faith
But honestly Ima need
for you all to stay in my lane
As spiritual speed bumps

I'm being real when I say
That often I get complacent
with speeding from day to day.......
.....thinking I know it all
and not eager to learn a thang....
.....nose higher and higher
not smelling my own stank
and then "blouw,"
Here go somebody
that really force me to think
So now they questioning Jesus
I instantly get defensive
Pride swelling up in me
I never notice until I'm finished
Sharp with the sarcasm
I slice and dice with precision
Instead of looking like Christ
I'm looking like a religion, that's why....

I need these people to check me
ruffle my waters forgive me
Father I'm horrible let me
see so much more of you
help me be whatchu taught me to be

a Warrior inside your oracle
fallin face to the floor for you

Lord can you please
help me keep my balance

(Verse 3)
Lord I don't wanna end up
stalling my light......
End up pausing my life
you've called me only to fight
and not end up Saul on my knife
but I see....
Me killing myself was all a part of my
Christ....
Sacrificing the body for better,
part of the price
he paid...
Attention to the fine details
we often overlook while looking in the mirror
we fail....ourselves, I know
I see it in me as I reveal
the inner parts within me
in a way that I won't derail...
I'm cheap scale
retail
weak frail
not strong enough for my own female
but..
That's why I need your unchanging strength

let's be real
look

My little brother's a teenager
and I see fear......
Not up in his eyes
but in me-self
I mean well
Lord..
Cuz I don't want him to be
another statistic..
Worse than he already is
because his fathers a nit...wit...
My father wasn't there so our whole
fatherly image
was twisted

But then you came Heavenly Father
and fixed it
but now...
I am a father
and a husband
and I'm struggling...
My ministry is thriving
but I'm fumbling my woman...
The rib you gave me
I have not loved her
the way you've summoned
and to know she feels less
than what she's worth
hurts my stomach......

...I'm disgusted at myself
she could do better...

I'm supposed to love my wife
like
Christ loved the church
When she looks me in my eyes
and tells me do better...
I get defensive
only making matters worse
Cuz I know that God
gave me a calling
and boy I'm on it....
Multi Award winner
and International Recording...
Artist
talkin bout Jesus
from Vegas to the Bahamas
But not a word about Him
while me and wifey in our pajamas
At the crib
watching old reruns of Martin Lawrence....
I promise you I'm only being honest...
She told me that she feels like she is second
to my calling
....and it's killing me because I know how she
feels
I caused it...
Lord I Need
BALANCE

Late 2019, heading into 2020, things were looking extremely promising for me.

My creative juices were flowing, and I was beginning to generate a buzz from some of my projects at that time. Not to mention, I had just come off of a promo tour which had me up and down the East Coast.

I had collaborated with a known artist from the CHH (Christian HipHop) community by the name of Jered Sanders, while making history in my hometown by being the first to ever shoot a music video in the gymnasium of our high school.

There was a lot of hype surrounding our project, and I was focused on using that energy to launch me into a better place for my overall career.

As all of this was occurring, my wife and I were in the worst place ever in our marriage.

January of 2020, she dropped a bomb on me that literally paused my entire life.

She made it clear to me that she was having thoughts of us pausing for a moment, in an effort to work towards getting our love back intact.

Truth be told, I was emptying myself into my ministry, while she caught the back-burner; needless to say, she was fed up with it.

While there were no mentions of divorce or anything to that extent, I knew that slight crack was all satan needed to try and shatter our union.

"Balance" came from a moment of serious reflection on my personal life, as well as the world around me at that time.

I began to notice a strong surge of people with my complexion standing firm against social injustices, while on the other hand, not highlighting the act of death we promote within our culture.

I noticed that the body of Christ was becoming more and more divisive towards one another due to personal opinions interfering with how Christ told us we should view one another.

I noticed how the more I gained knowledge from studying God's word, the more prideful I became in my desire to win whenever discussing Christianity with those who had opposing views.

Lastly, but definitely not least, I noticed how I was causing the woman I loved to question whether or not I was still "in love" with her.

God made it perfectly clear to me that *balance* is key in the life of the believer.

Without such an important tool, we are prone to wander aimlessly, basing our every decision off of our emotions and circumstances.

While it's natural for us to have emotions and experience circumstances, we are to hold God's word as the ultimate standard for our lives.

In other words, everything is to be weighed up against His word; from there, we use His word as our moral compass guiding us as we make our next move(s).

What this looks like is us knowing that God is justice, and His Holy Spirit is peace.

The two will only coincide when God is the centerpiece, because He cannot contradict Himself. In other words, if the spirit driving the fight for justice is not the Spirit of God, then His peace will not be seen on the receiving end, which truly exemplifies the saying, "No justice, no peace" ...because God is both.

What this looks like for the body of Christ is, until we equally hold God's word as our ultimate standard way of living, we will continue to dilute the sanctification amongst His believers.

Our personal feelings were never intended for us to use against one another; instead, they were meant to reflect the marvelous abilities of our God.

In other words, He snatched up people from all walks of life and placed His Holy Spirit within them, leaving them all on the same page, for the same purpose, while looking at things from different perspectives.

Yes, we are to remain unique in our own way, but being knit together by the Holy Spirit is what keeps us all in alignment with God's perfect will.

What this looked like for me, and my prideful way of evangelizing, is *1st **Peter Chapter 3 verses 15 and 16**,*

"..but sanctify Christ as Lord in your hearts, always being ready to make a defense to everyone who asks you to give an account for the hope that is in you, yet with gentleness and reverence; and keep a good conscience so that in the thing in which you are slandered, those who revile your good behavior in Christ will be put to shame."

At all times, I am to mirror God's love.

His second greatest commandment is to love our neighbors the same way in which we love ourselves.

The easiest way to lose a person for Christ is to beat them over the head with the Bible.

I am to never use God's word as a tool to belittle someone or bash them.

Instead, I am to use it to encourage, educate, and edify the person I'm engaging with.

To be specific, God's word covers all those bases itself, as stated in **2ⁿᵈ *Timothy Chapter 3 verses 16 and 17*,**

> *"All Scripture is inspired by God and profitable for teaching, for reproof, for correction, for training in righteousness; so that the man of God may be adequate, equipped for every good work."*

In one passage, you have a method of utilizing scripture to give a defense as to why you believe, while the other is built around discipling a fellow believer.

Neither, however, involve being argumentative and using knowledge as leverage to win a disagreement.

What holding God's word as the ultimate standard for my life also looks like is me loving my wife like Christ loved the church.

God requires intimacy, and that same intimacy is to be shown by a husband to his wife.

Holding God's word as the foundation of my marriage will ultimately place me and my wife's feet on Christ as we live, as one, to do His will.

*1st **Peter Chapter 3 verse 7** says,*

"You husbands in the same way, live with your wives in an understanding way, as with someone weaker, since she is a woman; and show her honor as a fellow heir of the grace of life, so that your prayers will not be hindered."

My wife should never have to question my love for her if I am truly loving her the way God has commanded me to in His word.

Regardless of how "successful" my music ministry may become, it is to never take precedence over my marriage.

God's establishment of marriage is a covenant, one that's far more important than any other ministry.

What He has joined together, let no man separate.

Those words have not been mentioned in regards to any other ministry He created.

Why not? Because marriage is to be a physical reflection of God's love for us.

Spiritual balance is a must for us to grow closer to God.

Without the understanding and application of balance, we can position ourselves to miss out on a deeper knowledge of God's plans for us as His children.

This song was written in an effort to express just how much more maturing I had to do in Him.

Chapter 5:

"My Pressure"

(Verse)
I be feelin just leave me alone
I be wanting to hide at my own home
I don't wanna talk I really don't
no
no
I just wanna calm my mind
Wanna turn off my line
I don't wanna know the time
You don't wanna know my why
It's my fault all the time
Feel so alone at times
Satan playin wit my mind
Open God's word to find
A lil bit of peace and quiet
I don't even feel like trying
If I didn't it would be a crime

There's a war going on inside
I never been the type
To let go of my pride
But it's killing me inside
Yea it's killing me inside

Got satan
all in my vision
seeing my enemy
as my wife
We both salty
at one another
tension thick could cut it
wit a knife
And I hate it
Lord knows I hate it
man I really hate it
when we fight
Cuz I'm always left
feeling guilty cuz
I'm supposed to love
her like Christ
Love the church......
Without blemish....
or spot
And that hurts......
I mean God
What about me.....
am I not
Supposed to feel weak....
I guess not

47

I be like please.....
make it stop
Change how I think.....
my God
You are my strength.....
all I got
Greater is you that's within me
I need to remember
when I'm going through it
and feel like submitting
I'm supposed to be trusting
in you not my feelings
I'm supposed to be resting
in you not my feelings
I'm supposed to be running
to you for the healing
My marriage is covered
your blood is what sealed it
.....Inside of your word is where
you revealed it
Quiet my life so your voice I can hear it
Increase within me Holy Spirit
while I deal with this

(Hook)
Pressure pressure
Pressure pressure
Pressure pressure pressure pressure
Pressure
Pressure pressure pressure
Pressure pressure

Pressure pressure
Pressure pressure pressure pressure
Pressure
Pressure pressure pressure
Pressure pressure
Pressure pressure
Pressure pressure pressure pressure
Pressure
Pressure pressure pressure
Pressure pressure
Pressure pressure
Pressure pressure pressure pressure
Pressure
Pressure pressure pressure

As a husband, it's often difficult to sit and reflect on your wrongs.

To have conversations of you and your wife replaying in your head days at a time can get pretty draining. This usually happens when things are extremely rocky between the two of you.

My wife and I were not in a good place whatsoever. Although I did not leave and we did not take the break that she felt we needed to take, we did seek spiritual guidance from our pastor and first lady.

Their godly counsel helped tremendously as we were both able to openly express ourselves.

My takeaway from those sessions, however, resulted in immense pressure.

Hearing her speak of the things that I was doing wrong, while knowing she was telling the truth, was tough.

Lack of intimacy, affection, spiritual leadership, and appreciation for her daily contributions as a mother and wife were just a few of the areas that I was slacking in.

During that time, my job had shut down due to covid; the weight of not being able to contribute to my family financially was eating me alive.

During all of this, I was a stay-at-home father, trying to make my music ministry my way of provision.

The problem, however, was that the harder I pushed to gain traction in that area, the further I was distancing myself from my family, both emotionally and spiritually.

While writing "Pressure," I was in a place of exhaustion.

Ironically, after writing and recording the song I felt better releasing those built-up emotions.

From listening to sermon after sermon, to studying daily devotionals, I noticed a constant trend in the information that I was receiving.

I began to realize that God had already equipped me with the tools needed to be the kingdom husband that my wife deserved.

I came to understand that it was on me to stay plugged in to Him and His word so that His guidance could be what led my family, and not my ambitions.

From there, I learned that it was a matter of obedience and how devoted I was to properly steward over what God had entrusted me with.

Chapter 6:

"My Obedience"

(Hook)
It's hard to obey
When I want my way
It's hard to obey
When I want my way
My obedience (is killin me)
Obedience (is killin me)
My obedience (is killin me)
Obedience (is killin me)
It's hard to obey
When I want my way
I get all in the way
When I want my way
My obedience (is killin me)
Obedience (is killin me)
My obedience (is killin me)
Obedience (is killin me)

(Verse 1)
Lord I am struggling
My mirror is suffering because of it
I know what to do but I don't wanna do it
I hate how I'm feelin I'm rummaging
Through excuses I'm left with these bruises
From killing myself I keep killing myself
Lord I really need help tired of feelin so
clueless
I'm through with the games.....
I'm through with the lames....
through with my brain....
I'm through with the sayings
I won't do it again....
then I do it again
Repenting but nothing is changing....
Livin so flagrant, up in y'all faces...
Like everything is ok when...
I know that I'm faking....bruh I be faking

Head up high feeling low tho....(low tho)
Asi Asi feelin so so....
I really need to pray but I won't tho
Knowing dag on well that I won't grow
Like this
it's a shame ain't it when I....
Know I'm supposed to run to You but how
can I....
I be feeling You don't wanna hear from me
then I....

53

Remember that no weapons formed
shall prosper
ABBA Father
Protect me from me.....
Protect me from me
you hear what I speak
You see what I do, Lord you even know what
I think
I don't have a clue how you do what you do
but my submission to you is weak....
I talk a good game
but walk like a lame
I need you to straighten my feet....
Direct them to you and your will.....
My faith in you tells me you will....
Replacing the way that I feel....
With hope that your word will prevail....
Because I know that you cannot fail....
I don't wanna be Jonah in the whale....
I need grace, I'm here at the well.....
....Living water submerge me
Heavenly Father
you know I be trippin for real

(Hook)
It's hard to obey
When I want my way
It's hard to obey
When I want my way
My obedience (is killin me)
Obedience (is killin me)

My obedience (is killin me)
Obedience (is killin me)
It's hard to obey
When I want my way
I get all in the way
When I want my way
My obedience (is killin me)
Obedience (is killin me)
My obedience (is killin me)
Obedience (is killin me)

(Verse 2)
Lord I am struggling
My mirror is suffering because of it
I know what to do but I don't wanna do it
I hate how I'm feelin I'm rummaging
Through excuses I'm left with these bruises
From killing myself I keep killing myself
Lord I really need help tired of feelin so
clueless
I'm through with the games.....
I'm through with the lames....through with
my brain....
I'm through with the sayins
I won't do it again....then I do it again
Repenting but nothing is changing....
Livin so flagrant, up in y'all faces...
Like everything is ok when...
I know that I'm faking....bruh I be faking

Lord, it's so easy to talk aboutcha....
Hard to look inside my mirror tho....
The fact, is I cannot talk withoutcha
But I'm finessing your grace like a finger-roll
You told me to fast, a month ago
I heard you so clear like a trumpet blow
Water....fruits and vegetables
But I'm eating pasta with chicken tho
Convicted I didn't know where to go
You are whatchu eat I was chicken bro
...I ran from you like you wouldn't know
...With disobedience I'm habitual
I'm sick of my sin and that's literal
My stomach in knots
a figure four
You're the physician I should get to know
....Because you know me
way better than I know myself
So I'm on my knees
Begging
Asking for mercy
Help me....
to forgive me...
cuz it's me
that hurts me
Holding my wrongs...
over my own head
from Thursday to Thursday
Lord, I am not worthy.....
but you find me worth it

(Hook)
It's hard to obey
When I want my way
It's hard to obey
When I want my way
My obedience (is killin me)
Obedience (is killin me)
My obedience (is killin me)
Obedience (is killin me)
It's hard to obey
When I want my way
I get all in the way
When I want my way
My obedience (is killin me)
Obedience (is killin me)
My obedience (is killin me)
Obedience (is killin me)

God's grace is unearned; however, directly neglecting to do something that God has instructed you to do is a different story.

I remember when I was out on tour back in 2017. The coordinator of the tour asked a rhetorical question that I will never forget.

His question was, "What's on the other side of your obedience?"

I was taken aback at how simple, yet complex, that question was.

The fact of the matter though, is that we will never know what's on the other side of our obedience, until we obey.

Over and over again, God was pricking me to have a more intimate relationship with Him. At that time though, my consistency was so inconsistent; whenever I was getting cold, He'd let me know.

I would stress more, or things would get rocky between wifey and I.

I'd also catch myself spending way too much time on social media, or just on my phone in general.

My mirror was clearly showing the person that was the biggest issue at that time.

I would catch myself talking *about* God more than I talked to Him.

My devotion time was at an all-time low, and I was feeling the effects of it as my activities during my downtime started to change.

I knew for a fact that I was devoting way too much time to social media, and at times, it almost felt like I was in bondage.

I would close the app, and in 20 minutes or so, I would find myself opening it back up and scrolling again.

I vividly remember the day I told my wife that I was being led to fast.

For 7 days I was to only have fruits, vegetables, and water.

I was eager to begin, and the very next day I instantly dove in.

Along with giving up all of the other foods I normally craved, I also gave up social media.

Sacrificing social media was definitely something that needed to be done.

Maybe 2 days or so into the fast, I found myself at Applebee's eating a grilled chicken alfredo bowl.

Not even 3 days in, and I was breaking my fast already.

I was honestly ashamed, and I kind of felt like God didn't want to hear from me; even my repentance felt empty.

This song embodies the turning point for me in this project.

It was here that I realized I was the problem in my overall growth.
God was trying to draw me closer to Him, but I was steadily refusing His fellowship while trying to achieve my ambitions, all while using His name.

As a married man with a family, I had to understand that there was far more than just myself attached to my obedience.

I was on a one-way street to blocking the blessings for my entire family.

It was safe to say, at that time, that I was my own thorn.

Chapter 7:

"My Own Thorn"

(Verse 1)
What would you call something that's
given to keep you in yo place
To keep you in yo lane
Humble, all throughout yo race
My mirror trippin cuz my ego do not know
that face
This pride of mines is hard to swallow
I don't like the taste
Be feeling like regurgitating throwing up my
set
Rap how I used to rap
throw some chains round my neck
Similes and metaphors demanding y'all
respect
My grandma house ain't have no porch
I jumped off the step

I grew up on them backroads, what do you expect
I know the ins and outs from A to Z without a sweat
I did it my way...that way no one could pose a threat
Living in circles....only Jehovah knows my reps
For many years
I've painted pictures with these words to flex
Those same years I hated living in that world of stress
I met a girl, looked in her eyes and all I seen was sex
I never thought I'd be my crucifix

(Intro)
I am my own thorn
I am my own thorn
I am my own thorn
I'm weaker than 7 days, receiving amazing grace...and still I manage to get up in my own way....
It's safe to say
I am my own thorn

(Verse 2)
Literally
That girl I met is now my wife it's getting clearer to see

God, ministering to me
throughout my moments of weakness He's
just tweaking these selfish lustful indecent,
tendencies that's within me I'm empty
but steadily runnin away from that Living
Water
which is proof
One could have tight flows wit loose screws
Them same ones writing providing you
skewed views
Could be them same ones beside you
providing a new noose look
I spent a decade not paying attention
giving my two cents
while desperate for recognition
Chest out not hearing nothing but my own
decisions
Prolly how I got all mixed up in that Mormon
religion
But God's conviction through the Holy Spirit
came and it witnessed
He took my years of confusion and washed it
clean with forgiveness
Giving this man you see today another
chance at His business
Which is what I'm supposed to be about
but without a doubt

(Hook)

I am my own thorn
I am my own thorn
I am my own thorn
I'm lying to my own face, relying on how I
think...while struggling with my emotions
getting in the way....
It's safe to say
I am my own thorn

(Verse 3)

It gets the heaviest
when you and wifey bumping heads
The kids are fed
but hella bored they want to play instead
They want attention while you trying to
suppress the inner stress that's within you so
you present
but not really there
.....and yeah...
I've got a knack for saying that I'm straight
While my body language screaming
please just get up out my face
Open the Bible tryna find a story to relate
then when I do it leaves me feeling like why
should I even pray
......or even write
what's the point if I ain't living right
These me-to-me discussions plague me
almost every night

Realizing this pride of mines is really who I'm
tryna fight
And Satan all up in my mind
relaxing with a glass of wine
My thoughts are asinine
depressing like half the time
The other half I'm fine
well atleast I think, I could be lying
How can this minister of the gospel
not be sound in mind

I thought His Jesus was his light
in all His darkest times
People say Christians are some hypocrites
well, they right
Cuz I don't know a perfect Christian
none of us are Christ
but what I do know is my walk with Yahweh
should suffice
because my efforts are attempts
To take away His shine
my inner demons are the evidence of this
I shouldn't be meddlin in His affairs He's said
if I'd just listen to His voice
and obey He'd take my weaknesses
and replace them with His strength
cuz by His strength I will survive
because I

Am my own thorn

I am my own thorn

I am my own thorn

I'm weaker than 7 days, receiving amazing grace...and still I manage to get up in my own way....

It's safe to say

I am my own thorn

In **2 Corinthians Chapter 12,** the Apostle Paul speaks of a thorn that was given to Him by God.

He stated that its purpose was to keep him humble, so that he wouldn't get boastful in what God was doing through him.

Although I could personally relate to that passage, it spoke to me a little differently. I was watching so many great things happen in regards to my music ministry, while witnessing my family life get rockier and rockier.

While I knew my balance was off and my obedience was teetering, I was still baffled when wifey and I would bump heads.

I'd always justify my actions in some form or fashion to make myself feel like I wasn't in the wrong.

I had read this passage before, and I had heard of it many times, but it never hit me like it hit me when reading it in 2019.

Paul's thorn was used to keep him in a place of submission to God.

Even when he begged God to remove it, God responded by telling him that His grace was sufficient for him, and that His power was perfected in weakness.

Through this passage, God was allowing me to see that as long as I continued to place my hands on the steering wheel of my life, I was going to continuously experience cycles of torment.

Once I realized this, I looked back over the years of my salvation up to that point.

I noticed how even in my early stages, I was more interested in taking the comfortable route; because of that, God would often have to do something drastic to get my focus back on Him.

I became a member of the Mormon church back in 2012, and I got saved in 2013.

Even then, I was negligent in reading and studying God's word.

Sure, I read the Book of Mormon, and parts of the other books that went along with that faith-system, but I never devoted a substantial amount of time in the Bible like God was nudging me to do.
Three years later, God convicted me like never before.

I was pierced to my heart at how ignorant I had become, and how disobedient I was being to His word.

Then and only then did I begin to study God's word, finding numerous contradictions between the Bible and the Book of Mormon.

Fast forward to 2019: I was married with two children, and a ministry that was thriving; at the same time, I was still negligent as it pertained to diving deeper into God's Word.

When He showed me that it was my blatant disobedience and lack of faith that was the blockage in my family's progression, it hit me like a ton of bricks.

I was taken back to the Apostle Paul, and how he pleaded with God to change His circumstances.

In my case, praying to God and asking Him to strengthen my marriage was a waste of time, seeing as I wasn't taking the steps He told me to take as a husband in relation to His word.

I wasn't studying to show myself approved, nor was I washing my wife with His word. When I read this passage, I instantly repented.

At that moment, I knew that the thorn in my flesh was me.

Chapter 8:

"Be Your Wind"

(Verse 1)
It's ironic how you have captured me
.I never would've pictured this
You seen me living so aimlessly
Yet
You targeted me with deliverance
My
Wife and kids are such a sight to see
But
They're not as beautiful as you Lord
Facts
I'm just grateful that I can finally see
That
You have so much more in store

Cuz Lord I know your promises
and on the other hand what you expect

From those who love you
they must live with the utmost respect
for your word
which are sometimes hard
but on God, only L I know is Lord

(Hook)
I just wanna be your....wind
Take me wherever you want, for me to go
I just wanna be your....wind
Together you and I gon blow
how high only you know
So I vow to you consistency and diligence
Never ever will you catch me on the bench
I just wanna be your....wind
You can take me wherever
Take me wherever
Take me wherever

(Verse 2)
And I mean it too
Cuz not one situation
have you failed to see me through
I be grinding but your grace is honestly the
fuel
Without your mercy my progress wouldn't be
visual
I bow before you wash your feet with my
beard
Cuz ain't no hair on my head
Lord I'm just tryna say I care

And I love you
So no matter the scenery I'm prepared
To give thanks
for your grace
praise your name
Cuz Lord I know your promises
and on the other hand what you expect
From those who love you
they must live with the utmost respect
Yeah
for your word
which you are sometimes it's hard
but on God, only L I know is Lord

(Hook)
I just wanna be your....wind
I'll go where you want for me to go
I just wanna be your....wind

Together you and I gon blow
how high only you know
So I vow to you consistency and diligence
Never ever will you catch me on the bench
I just wanna be your....wind
I just wanna be your....wind
You can take me wherever.....

At this point, I was determined to *show* God that I loved Him, as opposed to just making songs *about* loving Him.

I was tired of running away from His arms, and at the same time, dragging my family through it all.

I had so much to be grateful for; it was that understanding that created this song of worship.

I decided to no longer allow my own stagnant tendencies to defeat me spiritually, mentally, or physically; I declared to the Lord that I would be His win.

The play on the words win and wind were intentional.

Me saying "win" was a "send me, I'll go" kind of declaration; saying that I was ready and willing to be used for His purpose.

Me saying "wind" was to say how I would go wherever He wanted to take me, in complete submission to His leadership and devotion to His plan for my life.

I think of Isaiah when he had his own personal encounter with the Lord in *Isaiah Chapter 6.*

It was then that he recognized just how Holy God was, and just how corrupt he was really living in the eyes of God.

That realization ignited repentance in him that led to his submission and declaration to going and doing whatever it was that the Lord needed done through him.

This is a realization that we all must have in order to wholeheartedly respond to the calling of God on our lives.

We must first understand where we initially stood in the sight of God, and why we needed a Savior in the first place.

Once we understand our wretchedness, we are then faced with the choice of asking God to forgive us of our wrongdoings, which is repentance; or, we can try and live a life without repenting, and aim to be as good of a person as we can be, basing our goodness off of our own standards.

At that moment in my life, repentance and submission were exactly what I needed in order to properly hear from God.

Strengthening my sensitivity to His Holy Spirit was the game changer for me, my family, and my ministry.

He literally began speaking to me in a way that was clear, clean cut, and straight to the point. When you are close to God, His correction can sometimes feel like hate; however, the conviction you feel is His way of loving you into the path of His righteousness.

God will never step down from His throne of holiness in an effort to appease us in any way.

Instead, He will allow those who seek Him to witness His righteousness, so His Holy Spirit can correct them where they are.

Conviction is highly needed amongst the body of Christ.

Without that level of intimacy with the Holy Spirit, we run the risk of misrepresenting the image of our holy and righteous God.

Chapter 9:

"Conviction"

(Verse)
Watching passion of the Christ got me wanna fight
I'm tired of living this conviction got me wanna die
I'm tired of sinning in my mirror looking in my eyes
What is the reason I was chosen why do I have to try
I could've stayed the way I was
I wasn't happy but I was good
I mean I ain't grow up in no hood
Duckin shots from the opps or from the cops ain't have no pops but family that treated me good
Won't in no environment around no drugs no Crips or Bloods

And yea I smoked a lot of bud
popped bottles when I want
Different shorties I would cut
like I was good inside the mud
Lord I ain't need you to pick me up
But everything that you hearin
Is a 100% the reason that I needed to be
cleaned up
See I got comfortable in the mud
To the point it became a trend
It was cool to sleep with her
It was cool to think like him
It was cool to justify my wrongs and wipe it
off my chin
Adjust the brim
On my fitted kick up dirt then brush my timbs
But Lord you saved me
Lord God you saved me from that life
I had a daughter by my sin
but it was your love that gave me a wife
You redeemed me by
every drop of blood you sacrificed
Now I want my son, wife and daughter
seeing
you inside my eyes
You said to love you should be first
and everyone else second
You said I must die to myself
you knew I'd be my weapon

You said the wages of sin is death
so your crucifixion
Was payment for another
cuz you said you held no blemish
You said yo temple would be broken
in 3 days re-risen

And you said our bodies are a temple
we must see Your vision
The greatest cities in this world
required architects and blueprints
Our Architect was you Father
and blueprint is who You sent
Everything was written by yo Spirit
you have given us
The road map to life
to keep our lives away from trenches
Judas kissing on you
was a clear depiction of us Christians
See the Savior clear as day
but blinded to our hearts position
Many say they won't deny
make a vow to give they life
Sunday morning testify
then leave the church then go get high
Popping pills or bottles bruh the body got a
vice
Which I get because we're flawed
but see our vice supposed to be Christ
He suppose to be our liquor
He suppose to be our blunt

He suppose to be our porno
He suppose to be our punch
He suppose to be our fix
when we itchin for that bump
He suppose to be our answer
when it don't add up to sum
But we lookin like the world
Down playing what He's done
And as long as the body continues to waver
we will all be dim as one (yuh)

This is reproof
not condemnation
I'm just praying He would place us back in
the mud
rain down His saliva
Smear it over our eyes
So that we can see Him proper
in every situation
Spiritual war is what we're facing
No more hesitation
Cuz on everything Satan ain't playing
We need restoration
In drawing closer to our maker
No more procrastination
Cuz death ain't worried about your age
cuz when it's time
Then it's time
you are left with your decisions
You either chose heaven
or eternal separation

Conviction is essential to the growth of a believer, and a necessity to the lifestyle of the church.

Before writing this song, I was watching the movie "Passion of the Christ."

That movie puts me in a place of repentance every time I sit down and watch it.

The gut-wrenching desire to repent stems from the conviction I feel within.

Conviction can be easily defined as the awareness of sinful living.

Oftentimes, we compare ourselves to those around us. In doing so, we begin to subconsciously weigh the similarities and differences in our rights and wrongs.

By doing this, we tend to skip over the fact that we are all born in sin.

Conviction is the tool that the Holy Spirit uses to usher us into a deeper relationship with God.

Through conviction, we are shown our flaws in the sight of God, enabling us to face those mistakes and repent in an effort to receive God's forgiveness.

Ultimately, through conviction we receive salvation by confessing our flaws and accepting Christ Jesus as our personal Lord and Savior.

Leading up to that decision, conviction is what guides us to understanding why Jesus did what He did for us to begin with.

Without that personal understanding, there's no validity to your Christianity.

I was made to write this song in order to hold the church accountable for how loose we've become in our representation of our holy God.

I was also made to write this song to remind myself of the standard that God has set before me; a standard that will not waiver regardless of how long I go without listening to this song again.

If I ever begin to live a lifestyle contrary to God's standard way of living, this song will serve as the instrument to put me back in my place.

I would have never cared about God's heart, nor would I have desired any type of real relationship with Him, if it had not been for the Holy Spirit.

His Spirit of truth pricked my heart at a time when I needed it the most.

The conviction from that prick is what ignited an appreciation for His love.

Chapter 10:

"His Love"

(Verse 1)
I looked in the mirror and smiled
suhm I ain't done in a long time
man it's been a minute
since I opened up my issues
consolidated and started to deal wittem
from start to finish
My biggest hindrance is forgiveness of my
own self
I'd mess around and sentence me to life
Knowing daq on well I'm sorry
and my heart is not that type
Put my back against the wall
tossing turning every night
Drag my name, through the mud
wit these thoughts within my mind

I remember giving wifey hell for having a friend
Mainly cuz her friend won't a her, her friend was a him
Insecurities and pride, had me drunker than gin

Satan causing division all because I let him in
I was Jacob and Jonah wrestling God from within
I turned my back to my bible and started sippin again
Chasin a feeling that I knew only my God could provide
Pandora's box I opened but by His grace I survived

(Hook)
His Love
I can't explain His Love

(Verse 2)
From parking lot pimpin
To ministering in those same parking lots the difference
My heart posture have shifted
I was bought, specifically for my God to be lifted
I was created gifted....He saved me to be different

Jesus made it His mission to be relationship
driven
though He spake wit precision
few were able to vision
His intentions behind each parable
placed within them
Was the greatest wisdom
given here to stay for His children
The sheep know the voice of their shepherd

And He is not a respecter of persons
no one is greater or lesser
His guidance and his direction
is strictly for their protection
And every lesson that's given contains
multiple provisions
What is better buying fish, every day for your
son
Or buy him a pole
and show him how to catch himself one
We were given the Holy Spirit for the issues
to come
Enabling those with ears to hear
to not be spiritually numb

(Hook)
His Love
I can't explain His Love

88

I'm not the violent type at all
but being spit on would cause me to flip
blackout and serve damage
to whoever parted their lips
With every fiber of my being
I'd make'em pay for what they did
And they'd think twice before ever doing it
again

In the midst of retaliation
nowhere would my mind even consider
forgiveness
the two don't mix
oil and water
business is business
Even when it's all said and done
my heart would still be hard

But that's the difference
between me, and God
Cuz He suffered it all
And asked the Father to forgive the ones
beating on Him
As if they cared about the one they were
beating on
But seated on the throne
is compassion beyond measures
His purpose was to sacrifice His life
for His transgressors

A lion in His nature respectable in His
presence
At the same time a lamb and nothing short, of
precious
Yeshua
the ultimate prototype of perfection
Agape is His cologne
heaven scent for our direction .

(Hook)
His Love
I can't explain His Love
His Love
I can't explain His Love

I had heard of God's love, but I never really
understood the depth of it.

Having the Mormon faith as the foundation
that I was building my relationship with God
on was very confusing.

I was taught that the more I did in the name of
God, the more God would give back to me for
doing so.

So, I knew that God loved me because He
continuously woke me and my family up every
morning.

I still had it in my head and heart, however, that I deserved everything I had because of all that I was doing in and outside of my church; I even felt that way in regard to my own salvation.

There's a scripture in The Book of Mormon that really stood out to me during my time in that faith.

The scripture was **2 Nephi 25:23** which says, ***"For we know that it is by grace that we are saved, after all we can do."***

That verse played a significant role in my life.

While it was not as popular as **John 3:16,** or the others in the Bible that Mormons regularly recited, they lived it out on a daily basis and promoted that lifestyle within the theology.

The more I did, the less I focused on God's gracious love and what He'd already done for me.

That seed of confusion diluted my overall understanding of salvation.

Ephesians 2:8-9 states, *"For by grace are ye saved through faith; and that not of yourselves: it is the gift of God: not of works, lest any man should boast."*

Here, the Apostle Paul makes it clear that our salvation is a gift from God alone, through His grace and our faith.

What prompted a portion of my repentance during that time can be found at the end of these verses:

"Not of works, lest any man should boast."

This is the complete opposite of what the Mormon scripture stated at the end of their passage.

Their verse said, *"For we know that it is by grace that we are saved, after all we can do."*

Those five words at the end, *"after all we can do,"* changes the entire ideology of salvation.

The Holy Spirit had the Apostle Paul say that my works had nothing to do with God's decision in regards to my salvation, while the writer from the Book of Mormon told me that my efforts played a key role in my salvation because God's grace picked up the slack once my efforts ran short.

I began to see God's love for me through a different lens, one that removed me from the head of the picture and placed God where He belonged the whole time.

God's love for me is not contingent upon how much knowledge I have; he's not looking at how well I can walk into a room, grab a microphone, and handle a crowd.
He's not interested in my bank accounts or personal belongings.

He loved me before I was formed in my mother's womb; so much so that He included me in His plan for mankind to return back into His loving arms through the sacrificing of His only Son, Jesus the Christ.

He saw me fit to be sought after in the midst of many addictions; internally cleansed, having His grace be an eternal lotion that will never dry up.

As well as positioned in a place for His divine purpose while still here on earth, until I'm called home to be with Him in Heaven.

His love has shown me things that my natural mind would've never fathomed.

He has brought me through situations and circumstances that I wouldn't have made it through on my own.

His love is the catalyst for my faith; it keeps me grounded when my worry and doubt wants to take flight.

His love comforts me when I feel less than an adequate husband and father, and it reassures me that I am more than a conqueror in my moments of feeling defeated.

God's love is a love that I have learned to cherish; not necessarily because of what it offers me, but because I know it's genuine and pure.

Just thinking about His love makes me want to shout hallelujah!

Chapter 11:
"Hallelujah"

(Hook)
Halle.....lujah
Halle.....lujah
Halle.....lujah
Halle.....lujah
Halle.....lujah
Halle.....lujah
Halle.....lujah
Halle.....lujah

Praises going up
Blessings falling down
Ima lift Him up
And Ima hold Him down
I said
Praises going up
Blessings falling down

Down Down Down Down
Down Down Down Down

(Verse 1)
I do this for my G.O.D
(my G.O.D my God bruh)

Greater is He within me
(that 1 John 4:4)

I'm fishing intentionally
(Let's go)
The Word of God is sharp fileting the
adversary
I Came dripping covered by the blood
I was made from dirt so I get it out the mud
They be talking reckless I be like what's good
You don't want know problems get
calculatored
I'm no Patty Mayo get out my way Doug
I'm so underground your shovel wouldn't
touch
Imago Dei In Yahweh we trust
Living waters flowing from our
guts.....Yuuuhh

(Bridge)
Glory to the most high
You are worthy of all praise
And that is why I lift my hands to you
And Lord I wanna praise.....You

This is for the most high
Praises to the most high
And Lord I wanna praise.....You
Praises to the most high
(This is my worship)

(Hook)
Halle.....lujah
Halle.....lujah
Halle.....lujah
Halle.....lujah
Halle.....lujah
Halle.....lujah
Halle.....lujah
Halle.....lujah

Praises going up
Blessings falling down
Ima lift Him up
And Ima hold it down
I said
Praises going up
Blessings falling down
Down Down Down Down
Down Down Down Down

(Verse 2)
Look-a-here I came up
Came in this thang all stained up
Heart corrupted my brain bruh
But when God got up in that thang bruh

He made a
Way outta no way like ok
I done gave it to you now it's up to you and
your faith
Only thing I'm looking for in return
is your praise
Leave them other gods alone
they lower case
G's...weez...
see...we
Was under...water...
sea...weed
But came...up...
like Wee...zy
And George baptized in the name of the Lord
I.....I
I found Christ
Defeated death when I found life
That Holy Spirit in my sound byte
So worship is what I sound like
(Bridge)
Glory to the Most High
You are worthy of all praise
And that is why I lift my hands to you
And Lord I wanna praise...You
This is for the Most High
Praises to the Most High
And Lord I wanna praise...You
Praises to the Most High
(This is my worship)
(Outro)

My worship and praise comes from a place of remembrance.

I remember the guy I used to be prior to meeting Jesus.

I can recall my empty lifestyle, nights of depression, thoughts of suicide, even my attempts, all prior to God removing the scales from my eyes.

My hallelujah is my thank you to the God that left the ninety-nine and came searching for me, with only me in mind.

My music is my way of creating new ways to talk about God and introduce Him to others.

By using my personal testimony and God's Word about Himself, I aim to bring Him as much praise, glory, exaltation, and honor as possible.

"Hallelujah" was created to have the highest praise be sung aloud by all who would sing along to the catchy chorus.

In other words, whether the listener is a believer or not, as he or she sings the chorus to this song, they will essentially be celebrating our God in Heaven by giving Him the highest praise that can be given.

Throughout this song, I am speaking of the wretched man I used to be prior to God personally revealing Himself to me.

I stand today declaring that if my God does not do another single thing for me or my family, He is still worthy of my hallelujah, because of what He has already done!

Chapter 12:

"God's Got Me"

(Intro)
hand clap to this.....aye let me see ya hand
clap to this (hand clap to this)
hand clap to this.....aye let me see ya hand
clap to this (hand clap to this)
hand clap to this.....aye let me see ya hand
clap to this (hand clap to this)
hand clap to this.....aye let me see ya hand
clap to this (hand clap to this)

(Verse 1)
See I remember being all up in the world like,
oxygen and then my God, pulled me out, like
a splinter
I remember Him taking my pain like a
Vicodin and in Him, I could fall, like
November

Now da boy a son, of a king, call me Simba
Fight sin daily I'm a number one contender
Sick wit da flow Lord knows influenza
(Sick wit da flow Lord knows influenza)
ACHOO.....
Bless you, these lines and haikus come
straight from the heart through the dark to
find you
I rhyme to, invite Christ in ya life dude cuz I'd
like to, see y'all win like I do
(whooaah, whooaaah)
Aye look I am not egotistical God promised
the victory I agree with the spiritual....
That, mindset, is, a, must cuz only in,
Yahweh, I trust
Cuz I was looking to be held, in a cell, Up in
jail, or in hell, getting filled with the most
fire...
But now I'm aiming for the sky, with that fire,
in my eye, because I will reside, with the Most
High...
Cuz I was looking to be held, in a cell, Up in
jail, or in hell, getting filled with the most
fire...
But now I'm aimin for the sky, wit day fire, in
my eye, because I, will reside, wit da Most
High...

I ain't worried bout a thang (not a thang)
Cuz my God's Got Me (got me)
Yea my God's Got Me
I ain't worried bout a thang (not a thang)
Cuz my God's Got Me (got me)
Yea my God's Got Me
I ain't worried bout a thang (not a thang)
Cuz my God's Got Me (got me)
Yea my God's Got Me
I ain't worried bout a thang (not a thang)
Cuz my God's Got Me (got me)
Yea my God's Got Me

I ain't worried bout a thang (not a thang)
Cuz my God's Got Me (got me)
Yea my God's Got Me
I ain't worried bout a thang (not a thang)
Cuz my God's Got Me (got me)
Yea my God's Got Me
I ain't worried bout a thang (not a thang)
Cuz my God's Got Me (got me)
Yea my God's Got Me
I ain't worried bout a thang (not a thang)
Cuz my God's Got Me (got me)
Yea my God's Got Me

Got Me (got me)
Got Me (got me)
Got Me (got me)
My God's Got Me (got me)

Got Me (got me)
Got Me (got me)
Got Me (got me)
Yea My God's Got Me (got me)
I ain't worried bout a thang (not a thang)
Cuz my God's Got Me (got me)
Yea my God's Got Me
Yea my God's Got Me (got me)
My God's Got Me (got me)
My God's Got Me (got me)
God's Got Me

(Verse 2)
I'd be lying if I said otherwise hands up, to
the sky Lord can I get a witness
And if God's been good by your side, every
day and every night testify be a witness....
Boy....yea I luh, dat.....
I bet the angels in heaven really dug that....
I can see'em now, hittin da duggie
Whaaaaah They 2 steppin with a mug yeah
This type of.....praise and worship I love bruh
I give it all, to my God, up above bruh
Cuz He literally pulled me out of the mud
bruh
And then spiritually gave me something to
love bruh...
The Godhead 3 in 1 Father Spirit and Son
Is like ice water steam all 3 are 1 wheeew
(wheee)
That, there's, a must..

Because in, all 3 I trust
Cuz I was lookin to be held, in a cell, Up in
jail, or in hell, gettin filled with the most fire...
But I'm aimin for the sky, wit day fire, in my
eye, because I, will reside, wit da Most High...

Cuz I was lookin to be held, in a cell, Up in
jail, or in hell, gettin filled with the most fire...
But I'm aimin for the sky, wit day fire, in my
eye, because I, will reside, wit da Most High...

(Hook)
I ain't worried bout a thang (not a thang)
Cuz my God's Got Me (got me)
Yea my God's Got Me
I ain't worried bout a thang (not a thang)
Cuz my God's Got Me (got me)
Yea my God's Got Me
I ain't worried bout a thang (not a thang)
Cuz my God's Got Me (got me)
Yea my God's Got Me
I ain't worried bout a thang (not a thang)
Cuz my God's Got Me (got me)
Yea my God's Got Me

I ain't worried bout a thang (not a thang)
Cuz my God's Got Me (got me)
Yea my God's Got Me
I ain't worried bout a thang (not a thang)
Cuz my God's Got Me (got me)
Yea my God's Got Me

I ain't worried bout a thang (not a thang)
Cuz my God's Got Me (got me)
Yea my God's Got Me
I ain't worried bout a thang (not a thang)
Cuz my God's Got Me (got me)
Yea my God's Got Me
Got Me (got me)
Got Me (got me)
Got Me (got me)
My God's Got Me (got me)
Got Me (got me)
Got Me (got me)
Got Me (got me)
Yea My God's Got Me (got me)
I ain't worried bout a thang (not a thang)
Cuz my God's Got Me (got me)
Yea my God's Got Me
Yea my God's Got Me (got me)
My God's Got Me (got me)
My God's Got Me (got me)
God's Got Me (got me)
Got Me (got me)
Got Me (got me)
Got Me (got me)
My God's Got Me (got me)
Got Me (got me)
Got Me (got me)
Got Me (got me)
Yea My God's Got Me (got me)
I ain't worried bout a thang (not a thang)
Cuz my God's Got Me (got me)

Yea my God's Got Me
Yea my God's Got Me (got me)
My God's Got Me (got me)
My God's Got Me (got me)
God's Got Me

"God's Got Me" came from a place of declaration.

I remember when COVID-19 was first announced, and I watched how fear was sweeping the world around me.

I remember telling my wife how I wasn't worried, nor was I going to panic or stress; I knew God said in His word that He'd be my refuge and my fortress if I abode in Him.

So, I openly declared by faith that the world around me could do what they felt they had to do, but as for me and my house... we were going to stand on the Lord's promises over our lives.

It's very easy to sing along to a song like this, and yet live contrary to what you are declaring.

In knowing that, I gave listeners an example of how to use what they've been through in order to catapult their faith into action.

I remembered the life I once lived, and recalled how God's eyes never left me, even in the midst of my mess.

I can honestly say that He thought enough of me to create in me a new heart and a new way of life.

It's those moments of gratitude that ought to be celebrated and declared unto others.

If God does nothing else for me in life, He's already done enough, and will be forever worthy of my praise.

Chapter 13:

"All By Myself"

(Hook)
I can never let my grip, go
Hold on til my breathe, gone
You will never make me slip, no
You ain't fittna bring me there bruh
I can do bad all by myself, tho
(I can do bad all by myself, tho)
I can do bad all by myself, tho
Iont need yo help, no
I got suhm to live, fo
Household and my kin, folk
God got me like 10, 4
You ain't fittna trick me up bruh
I can do bad all by myself, tho
(I can do bad all by myself, tho)

I can do bad all by myself, tho
Iont need your help, no

(Verse 1)
There's power all up in my tongue...
Confessing that I will not be defeated
And If God, with me why run
Is what I'm asking myself when I feel the
weakest
....At times, feel like I am on the bleachers....
In timbos...... not even sneakers
Tho the rents due whip need Petro and my
chips low all I need is Jesus
Enemy coming after me and my family tryna
make me put my light down
But the Holy Spirit residing in the inner me
got me ready for the fight now
But when Jesus , stepped outta the grave, we
got the victory so basically right now
There is nothing you can do to stop us we're
heirs, to whatever is His, so pipe down
You coward, you got no power, you take
more L's than Snoop do
We all W's wit it like Snoop dude we don't spit
Crip no bluetooth
Only rep the blood but no soo woop give em
straight Word like doop doop
My pedigree is on woof woof cuz my God
reigns till the roof loose

111

(Hook)
I can never let my grip, go
Hold on til my breathe, gon
You will never make me slip, no
You ain't fittna bring me there bruh
I can do bad all by myself, tho
(I can do bad all by myself, tho)
I can do bad all by myself, tho
Iont need yo help, no
I got suhm ta live, fo
Household and my kin, folk
God got me like 10, 4
You ain't fittna trick me up bruh
I can do bad all by myself, tho
(I can do bad all by myself, tho)
I can do bad all by myself, tho
Iont need your help, no

(Verse 2)
I'm no longer avoiding the smoke
I pray in the Spirit give me atleast 20 minutes
Boy I'm going for broke
The riches I was given is for me to pay
attention
Wutchu all on me fo
But I get it I'm a threat to you Satan so
typical
Hate is your ritual corny and pitiful weak in
the physical weak in the spiritual seven
days.....
Weaker than seven days.....

You can get hit up like seven ways.....
Straight up the gut like I'm seven Rays
when He touchdown you'll see heavens rays
1-2 with an unleavened taste
...Giving praise till the heaven's raised
Steppin boldly in the devils space and A-
Town stumping on the devil's face mortal
kombat but I'm Luke Cage
..... double edged with 2 blades
Baraka like in the Dark Knight I am walking
light go from Lui Kang into Bruce Wayne
you'll get saufleed
...... sins payment is your doomsday
Boy I rep Christ my death is life so I'm
straight regardless of what you think real
talk

(Hook)
I can never let my grip, go
Hold on til my breathe, gon
You will never make me slip, no
You ain't fittna bring me there bruh
I can do bad all by myself, tho
(I can do bad all by myself, tho)
I can do bad all by myself, tho
Iont need yo help, no
I got suhm ta live, fo
Household and my kin, folk
God got me like 10, 4
You ain't fittna trick me up bruh
I can do bad all by myself, tho

113

(I can do bad all by myself, tho)
I can do bad all by myself, tho
Iont need yur help, no
I can never let my grip, go
Hold on til my breathe, gon
You will never make me slip, no
You ain't fittna bring me there bruh
I can do bad all by myself, tho
(I can do bad all by myself, tho)
I can do bad all by myself, tho
Iont need yo help, no
I got suhm ta live, fo
Household and my kin, folk
God got me like 10, 4
You ain't fittna trick me up bruh
I can do bad all by myself, tho
(I can do bad all by myself, tho)
I can do bad all by myself, tho
Iont need your help, no

The only power satan has is what we give him.

He is, and always will be, under our feet.

Why? Because of God's living presence inside of His believers.

Through His spirit, we are able to take the stance of dominance over satan as well.

My aim in this song was to paint, as vivid as possible, how conniving, cunning, and weak satan truly is.

Faith in Christ alone gives us authority that satan will never receive.

The main thing about it is Satan knows the power we have through Christ Jesus, and that's why he is determined to distract, discourage, and attempt to deter us from carrying out God's will.

By ourselves, we are no match for satan; however, when we utilize God's living Word in accordance with His Holy Spirit, there's not an enemy in the earth who can defeat us.

We are more than conquerors through Christ Jesus our Lord.

By using metaphors, a catchy hook, and a dope beat, I made it my mission to make it plain and clear that satan will not have any influence over me or my household.

Whatever wrongs committed in my home will be on account of our own personal slip-ups and falling short.

Satan will have no place in our dwelling.

Chapter 14:
"G.O.E. pt. 4"

(Verse)
One time for the spark that was lit
Jesus Christ took my heart that was it
no more tug of war
He had a firm grip yanked the rope
A young Jonah I almost sank the boat
My water walking days started faith in God
done got me chasing hope
Gary Payton how I plays Him close
It's Christ Jesus the Lamb...
Yeshua when I thank the g.o.a.t
Remain low until exalted His name I boast
Set fire to any track so His name I toast call it
communion
We on one accord no Ford Fusion
I'm built Lord tough for this thang no joke

So set aside the lols and miss me wit tha
fugazi I'd rather after a show you go repent
instead of pay me
I know the industry say that don't make
cents.....
And it don't
but I'm more worried about your soul
discipleship is the goal, look
I veered off bag chasing in that clout game
Seeking features for they name tryn scout
fame
Money lookin Kevin Hart funny
and then the doubt came
Tryna force out brainstorms within a
drought mane
Tryn to assure that ya boy had a devout
name
.......mane......I was lost in the sauce
.....leaving puddles of pride with every step I
was off
Aiming for God's heart and completely
missing the mark
......9:24 my unbelief is an of-course
Even tho I believe and I proudly accept my
cross
I'd be lying if I say that I never have second
thoughts
Picture me, on the boat with Jesus thinking of
jumping off
when the waves got rocky and suddenly came
the storm

117

...........it's transparency I'm tryna talk to you
.......Humble myself make time and walk to you
.....kill my flesh and then hand chalk to you
I am blessed....and not for reasons materialistic
Jesus died and He rose for my transgressions
Walking from, city to city through county lines defying minds that couldn't comprehend Him being the Messiah
....they needed sign after sign besides the ones before they eyes
And they was with Him like 95, percent of the time
His disciples, seeing all that and still blind
Sorta like me in my mirror examining what you hide look, look
.....those who have ears let em hear
Your eyes might lie to you and ya heart don't think clear
Get outcho feelings...and into my presence
A present day revelation given directly to me from the Holy Spirit
I was stressing.....pride digesting body rejecting
Indigestion, spiritual war in my mid-section
My own daughter said I looked like a pile of depression
....tho I knew she was joking inside my blood it was boiling

Angry because the feeling I was feelin was so controlling
........yea, then I remembered it was spoken
That in my weakness His strength is made whole
So any victory I gain is through His blood and not my own
....yea....I'm 8 ball corner pocket
but I'm coming off the reel with every line I fish
I pray more when that conviction hits and that conviction hints
I've fallen short, in His eyes again
But there He go amazing grace how sweet the sound
That saved a wretch like me from that ol E-Town
Miller's Tavern, I-Neck is where my home be found
With that said, I don't expect home to hold me down nah
A new creation not the same ol guy
I've changed no lie I don't do this for the fame nor vine
My flame for God I'm praying that it stay on fire
No chip on my shoulder I don't want no Frito Lays no sah
They sleepin on Christ, iont entertain those lies
I'm team G, never ever will I play both sides

My bets on Yeshua the rest, I just pay no mind
It's GOE, God over everything fo' life, Rock

Summarizing everything that took place during the time of making this album and putting it all in one song was nothing short of God revealing Himself and His abilities.

I first fell in love with the beat to this song because it gave me an old Jay-Z vibe; those who truly know me know that Jay-Z was one of my biggest musical influences growing up.

When I began writing, however, I could instantly feel God speaking.

My thoughts were connecting so easily, and the flow of the imagery was a lot smoother than normal.

I could instantly tell that this song was going to make for the perfect closing piece for the album as a whole.

What I didn't know, however, was just how deep Holy Spirit was going to dig into the process.

Throughout my musical journey, I've found myself going through several internal challenges; I've wrestled with pride, and the desire to be recognized plagued my mind during the majority of those years.

Now granted, there's nothing wrong with seeking to make a name for yourself in your craft; the slope, however, becomes slippery once you incorporate pride into the mixture of your heart's desires.

It got to where I could no longer celebrate others in their moments of success without feeling like I deserved what they had received.

I got so prideful to where it was difficult for me to listen to certain artists, because instead of me hearing the gospel message in their songs, I was infatuated with comparing myself to them as an artist.

I began making it my mission to save up money and pay some of the bigger names in the industry to collaborate with me.

This wasn't done with the heart posture of coming together to strengthen God's kingdom on earth; instead, I wanted to give off the idea that I had gotten to a certain level in my career where I could get these people on a track with me.

I went from trying to find my identity as a young adult amid a culture full of clones, to now using Christ to establish an identity based out of my pride and selfish ambitions. Because of doing this, I began falling out of love with my craft, which in turn, became a stumbling-block to me using my gift to push the gospel.

The title of this song is G.O.E pt.4, which stands for "God Over Everything."

The initial idea behind this particular series was to bombard the listener with heavy wordplay and metaphorical imagery, all the while drilling how God was to never be second.

In the parts leading up to number 4, I expressed how solidified my stance was in Christ.

Each song sounded different as the beats gave off a different feel, while I conveyed the message precisely and strongly.

I aimed to use as much of the instrumental provided to show just how corrupt the industry was, how confused and misguided the mentality of those opposing the gospel were, and how significant Christ is to the culture(s) around us.

Part 4 was different because God literally had me writing it as if I were looking in a mirror. Every bar was a recap of my heart's posture, as He kept pulling out more and more things that I wasn't expecting to put to a beat.

As I previously mentioned, my thoughts were connecting much easier; however, this was honestly predicated upon my submission, meaning I literally had to write down the initial thoughts that came to my mind.

This was literally how the entire writing process took place for this whole album.

The more I allowed myself to say what God wanted to say, the deeper each song got.

G.O.E. pt.4 was the perfect final piece because it came out summarizing the album as a whole, while still holding true to the original scheme of the series. God Over Everything.

Keep in mind that in this case, I wasn't exposing the culture, but instead, I was exposing myself.

Chapter 15:

"Outro"

If you've made it this far in your reading, then aside from me thanking you for your time, I'd like to leave you with a question.

Who are you outside of God?

I believe the easiest way to answer that question is to first know who you are in God; and by God, I mean Christ Jesus.

It has to be made clear that Jesus the Christ is God Himself.

That cannot be up for debate, nor something that our faith is shaky on.

The Apostle John shows us in the **book of John** that Jesus is fully human and fully God.

In **Chapter 1 verse 1** John says, ***"In the beginning was the Word. The Word was with God and the Word was God."***

Skipping down in the same chapter, but to **verse 14,** John then states, ***"And the Word became flesh, and dwelt among us. We observed His glory, the glory as the one and only Son from the Father, full of grace and truth."***

With John being one of Jesus' 12 disciples, he spoke from the position of being an eyewitness to Christ.

Jesus himself says in **John Chapter 10 verse 30,** *"I and the Father are one,"* while Paul makes it crystal clear to the church in Colosse in **Colossians Chapter 1 verse 15** by referring to Jesus as ***"the image of the invisible God."***

Solidifying the fact Jesus Christ is God in our hearts allows us to better receive His words as authoritative over our lives, thus making what He says the standard by which we live.

Once we are secure in that area, we can then begin to understand who we are in Him.

The keyword in that sentence, however, is "we," because there's two audiences we're discussing here.

You have the believers on one side, and the unbelievers on the other.

God makes it very clear in His Word where both parties stand in His eyes.

To the believers, He calls us His children, His sheep, heirs, a royal priesthood, conquerors, salt of the earth, image-bearers, ambassadors, a peculiar-people, a chosen generation, and the list goes on and on.

To the unbelievers, however, our holy and righteous God calls them to repentance.

The Apostle Peter said in **2nd Peter Chapter 3 verse 9,** *"The Lord is not slack concerning His promise, as some count slackness, but is longsuffering toward us, not willing that any should perish but that all should come to repentance."*

God's heart is for all of His creation to return back to Him, and the only way to do so, is to fully believe in Him.

He has made Himself available in every way possible; from leading and guiding His people through different elements in which He saw fit, to lowering Himself in the form of a human being here on earth, and then finally awakening His spirit within the body of the believer allowing them to carry out His great commission after His death, resurrection, and ascension.

All of this was done so that no one would die and spend eternity separated from God.

He is not confined by time; time is just another creation of His that He uses as He sees fit.

With us, time is something that we are bound by; time is something that we chase after while never being able to grasp it.

That time is God's grace and mercy being bestowed upon us; to the believer, in a way that he or she can fully carry out all that God has entrusted them to complete.

While to the unbeliever, time is God's grace and mercy in a way that they can humble themselves and see that we are all flawed individuals who make mistakes, which breaks the heart of a perfect and holy God.

It's only through our faith in Jesus Christ alone that we are cleared of all charges.

We are then spiritually freed from our past wrongs, granting us a new life in Christ.

The genuine acceptance of this life looks the same through those who truly desire to love God.

As they continue to dive deeper and deeper into God Himself, through His word, the "believer" will then begin to transform internally, thus changing what they look and act like externally.

True followers of Christ live in a way of desiring more of the things that honor God, instead of the things that honor themselves.

By doing this, they take on the cross of Christ as a lifestyle.

Christ Jesus Himself, in agonizing pain and grief, said in **Matthew Chapter 26 verse 39,** *"O My Father, if it possible, let this cup pass from Me; nevertheless, not as I will, but as You will."*

Jesus was submitted to what the Father wanted Him to do, even when at that present time it wasn't what He truly desired.

That's what it means to be an image-bearer of Christ.

We not only reflect Him in our triumphs, but also in our struggles, through submission to God's divine plan.

"Lord, if this is what you want me to go through, then give me the strength to stand in You and endure; help me to see what lesson I am to learn by enduring this."

The transforming power of Jesus Christ changed, and is still changing me, as I continue to grow in Him.

I know for a fact what it looks and feels like to not believe in God.

I know the emptiness and confusion that it brings; especially to a young person that's trying to find out who they are becoming as an adult.

I stand 10 toes solid in saying that I know what it looks and feels like to know who I am in Christ Jesus.

I am literally no longer controlled by the desires that I once had, and I have a spiritual activator (Holy Spirit) on the inside of me, leading me into all truth.

I don't claim to be a theologian, nor do I have the knowledge of one, but I do have a testimony that is steadily getting stronger and stronger each and every day that God allows me to wake up.

Because of that fact alone, I am determined now more than ever to share the gospel of Jesus Christ, along with my testimony, to the world – using whatever method God gives me to use.

Through His amazing grace, my voice will reach those who it's intended to reach, and I pray that whatever mark I leave on this earth, resembles His holy and righteous standard.

Dear Father,

The seeds have been planted.

My prayer at this point is one of thankfulness.

Thank You, Lord, for allowing this book to cross this person's path during this time in their life.

Thank You, Lord, for allowing this person to read this far.

Thank You, God, for sectioning off their attention and drawing them into what You wanted them to hear.

Thank You, Lord, for entering the heart of this person and taking up residence.

Thank You, God, for ministering to them by using the different areas of my life that they could personally relate to.

Thank You for what you are doing on the inside of them, Lord.

Thank You that the people that are connected to them will benefit from the spiritual transformation that you are creating within them, Lord.

Thank You, Father, for strengthening them in You so they can go forth and boldly tell the world about Your gospel, Lord.

Thank You for removing all evil away from them, God.

Thank You for increasing their sensitivity to the things that disturb You, Lord.

Thank You for intensifying Your conviction, thus drawing them closer to Your heart, Lord.

Thank You for opening them up to the possibility of a better life in You, God.

Thank You for being patient with them, Lord.

Thank You, God, for the amazing grace and mercy You've shown to them thus far, Lord.

Thank You for revealing Yourself to them, whether they've noticed You yet or not, Lord.

With that being said, thank You in advance for opening their spiritual eyes so that they can begin to see You clearly in all things, Father God.

Thank You for allowing the words in this book to ignite a flame inside of them, God.

Thank You for being their peace as they embark on this journey with You, Lord.

Thank You for increasing their faith in Your Word as they see it come to life through the world around them, Lord.

Thank You, God, for being real to them; for being relevant to them, Lord God, thank You for providing for them in the capacity in which You see fit.

Lord, thank You for literally blessing this person, and equipping them with what's needed so they can further expand Your Kingdom here on earth.

I say all of these things in the name of my savior, Yeshua (Jesus) the Christ, AMEN.

Chapter 16:

"The Breakdown"

"See I begin every day with faith my ends meet"

(Transparency pg. 9)

1. I start off my day believing that I will see it completely through.
2. I approach every day with faith that I will be financially sufficient regardless of what the day entails.

"The Alpha and, the Omega's who I then seek

First that's why His Spirit's what you're hearing when my pen leak"

(Transparency pg. 9)

1. I seek spiritual guidance from the Lord, and it's His instruction that I write in my songs.

"Drowning in my sin had me tippy-toeing six feet"

(Transparency pg. 9)

1. In comparing the extent of my sinful living to a swimming pool, I had to tippy-toe in the 6-ft section due to the height of my sin almost taking me under. In other words, with the life I was living, I barely made it out alive, so I had to elevate in order to survive.

"Till God showed me that it's He who opens doors so

Now to level up I twist the handle like a six speed"

(Transparency pg. 9)

1. Since no elevation in life comes without God's gracious provision, I now walk into any upgrade by way of His entrance.
2. Six speed bicycles have their gears on the right handlebar in which twisting it upwards increases the intensity of the gear, thus elevating your speed.

In comparison, God's grace is what allows me to twist any doorknob in life and elevate from that current state I'm in prior to doing so.

"Mad cologne trying to hide the loud scent

Cuz money talks and I ain't have to ask Chris Tucker or Charlie Sheen"

(Transparency pg. 9)

1. "Loud" here is referring to strong weed, as well as a strong or intensified audible.
2. "Scent" is referring to smell, along with cent, as in a penny.
3. "Loud scent" and "money talks" play on one another, because the "loud cent" would refer to the "money talking."
4. Chris Tucker and Charlie Sheen were mentioned because of the quadruple entendre that was used on their 1997 movie title "Money Talks".

"Youngin outta the hiccups now I'm swallowing truth

Regurgitating the facts giving you the good fruit

Cuz the body needs its nourishment

I've been given the juice

So when I concentrate

my squeeze is being put to good use"

(Transparency pg. 11)

1. The "hiccups" are compared to my constant shortcomings.
2. Hiccups typically hinder one from being able to swallow or speak in the moments of them happening. Here, I express how God took me out of the lifestyle of constant "hiccups," or mishaps, thus allowing me to "swallow," or spiritually take in, His truths.
3. "Regurgitation" is when undigested or partially digested food comes back up from the esophagus. The food still has its normal taste and is not acidic due to it having not yet entered into the stomach.

4. Me regurgitating the facts of the spiritual truths God allowed me to take in made it so that I was passing on good fruit to those with ears to hear.
5. Those with ears to hear would technically be the believers, or aka "the body" of Christ.
6. Still playing off of the "good fruit" scheme, the nourishment from fruit typically lies within the juice, which is also called the "concentrate."
7. The play on "squeeze" is to symbolize the pressure I apply in my craft, along with what is essentially done to fruit in order to get the bulk of the nutrients out of it.
8. The overall idea is me saying that God removed me from a lifestyle of constant mistakes, and placed me in a position to spiritually eat His truths. In doing so, I zealously began to share what I was learning to fellow believers in attempts to help strengthen the body of Christ.

"It's all facts no printers"

(Transparency pg. 11)

1. The word "facts" is being compared to "fax."

"I'd rather trust Acts than pretenders"

(Transparency pg. 11)

1. On one hand, "Acts" is referring to the book of Acts in the Bible, while it's also a play on words, referring to "acts," which incorporates actors, or pretenders.
2. The overall message is to say that I'd rather trust the word of God over anyone else.

"My sword is like an ax for the splinters"

(Transparency pg. 11)

1. Based off of Ephesians 6:17, my "sword" is the Word of God.
2. Still playing on the word "acts," however this time I'm saying "ax."

3. "Splinters" has a double meaning; one meaning paints the picture of an ax cutting a splinter, which we know that splinters are very small.
4. The overall message here is to give a visual of just how mighty God's word is; it's like chopping a splinter with an ax.

"The map gave His life and His back and took crack after crack for us sinners"

(Transparency pg. 11)

1. "The map" here is in reference to Jesus Christ, because in John 14:6 Jesus told Thomas, "I am the way, the truth, the life. No one comes to the Father except through me."
2. Overall, Jesus not only gave His life, but He also suffered physically in order to redeem us of our sins. It's only through belief in Him that we can return to the Father.

"Everybody talking bout the plug

never was I ever that guy"

(Breathe pg. 16)

1. "Plug" is a slang term for drug-dealer.

"Lowkey wit my own crew

'09 living like '02"

(Breathe pg. 17)

1. "Lowkey" means to not be out loud or over-the-top; discrete or in secret.
2. "09 living like 02," basically means that in 2009 I was still living with the same mindset I had back in 2002.

"young-minded

Immature

Marques Houston"

(Breathe pg. 17)

1. A definition for the word immature is for one to be young-minded.
2. Immature was also a boy band in the 90's whose lead singer was Marques Houston.

"30 on'em with the pen

sweet wit da flow need insulin"

(Breathe pg. 17)

1. "30 on'em with the pen," speaks of me writing from a grown man state of mind.
2. "Sweet" has a double meaning. One speaks of how I am lyrically gifted.
3. The other refers to sweet in a way of a diabetic needing an insulin pen.
4. "Pen" also has a double meaning; one being an actual pen that you write with, and the other being an insulin pen.

"I was stealing liquor gettin zoot"

(Breathe pg. 18)

1. Zoot is a slang term meaning to be drunk and high at the same time.

"Me and Killa Leta on the step"

(Breathe pg. 18)

1. Killa Leta is a neighborhood friend from my late teenage years.

"I was living foul like roughing the kicker"

(Gotta pg. 23)

1. The word "foul" has a double meaning.
2. While the word "foul" means vile or disgusting, it's also a sports term for plays such as "roughing the kicker," which are unacceptable acts resulting in a penalty.

"throwing up E-Town wit a cup full of liquor"

(Gotta pg. 23)

1. The play on words here is the term "throwing up."
2. "E-Town" is a nickname for the county where I was raised. Residents from the area would make the letter E with their fingers and throw it in the air.
3. For some, a full cup of liquor may cause them to throw up.

"blunt smelling loud got thump in the Swisher"

(Gotta pg. 23)

1. The slang definition for "loud" refers to weed being potent or strong; hence why it says, "smelling loud."
2. The original definitions for both "loud" and "thump" include a strong audible sound.
3. A swisher is a type of cigarillo that's commonly used to roll up weed.

"Hard to keep my feet down

I was up in the middle of confusion"

(Gotta pg. 23)

1. The words "down" and "up" are being played on here.
2. Typically, when both feet are down it means you are standing still; my constant activity at that time kept me in the middle of the wrong things.

"It's getting heavy, my shoulders bulging"

(Balance pg. 30)

1. Typically, the heavier the weight is that one lifts, the bigger and stronger the muscles targeted get.

"Tho I'm not giving up this pressure's got my dawgs barking gottem talkin...."

(Balance pg. 30)

1. The slang term "got my dawgs barking" means that one's feet are hurting.
2. My persistence to overcome is the reason my feet are hurting.
3. The play on words here is the term "dawgs," because I'm also referring to them as "my homies."

"The elephant inside the room I now can see is heartless.....

Sin......."

(Balance pg. 30)

1. The definition for "the elephant inside the room" means an obvious major problem or issue that people avoid discussing or acknowledging.
2. The word "heartless" is being played on to mean both uncaring, as well as to literally not have a heart, meaning not alive.
3. The definition for "sin" is a transgression against a divine law.

4. In Genesis Chapter 3, sin was first introduced into human history by way of Adam and Eve deliberately disobeying God and eating from the only tree He did not give them access to eat from.

Sin does not have a body, nor is it able to make decisions on its own. It is a spiritual force that surfaces through the actions of human beings.

Ephesians 6:12 reads, "For our struggle is not against flesh and blood, but against the rulers, against the authorities, against the cosmic powers of this darkness, against evil, spiritual forces in heavenly places."

With that being said, the root cause of a lot of the problems we face as human beings does not begin with other human beings. Sin is the culprit; however, it's rarely addressed because most people refuse to focus on the spiritual, thus allowing it to be the "elephant in the room" in most situations.

"Send......

Me back to the garden where Adam corrupted Heaven's dream....."

(Balance pg. 31)

1. Although heaven is not an actual person and cannot technically dream, the implication being made here is one that lies within Genesis chapters 1, 2, and 3.

   In Genesis Chapter 1, God made a man and gave him dominion over all the fish of the sea, the birds of the sky, the livestock, the whole earth, and the creatures that crawl on the earth.

   In Genesis Chapter 2, God reveals the man's name as being Adam, and gave him a home, which was the Garden of Eden.

   In Chapter 3, however, Adam did not exercise his dominion and allowed satan, embodied as a snake, to trick and persuade his wife, Eve, into disobeying God's command.

2. Overall, God's original intent was for Adam to have dominion over all that God gave him, thus allowing him to be and remain in perfect fellowship with God. Due to his neglect and blatant disobedience, however, sin surfaced and contaminated the world from there on out.

"Our insecurities look Moses-like we need an Aaron"

(Balance pg. 31)

1. In Exodus Chapter 3, God speaks to Moses through a burning bush and assigns him the task of freeing the Israelites from the Egyptians.

   Moses' responses came from a place of personal insecurities and feelings of inadequacy.

   When God told Moses to speak with Aaron and have Aaron go with him on the assignment, there's no context mentioning of Aaron responding the way that Moses did.

2. The overall meaning is saying that instead of allowing our insecurities to deviate us from, or cause us to question God's assignment for us, we need to have less of a Moses approach and more of an Aaron approach.

"Initiate you learning you that should not be an errand"

(Balance pg. 31)

1. The significant thing about an errand is that it's typically a task that's being fulfilled for someone else.
2. The overall meaning is that when it comes to initiating the process of us knowing who we are, it should not be predicated on appeasing anyone other than God.

"Full of ourselves

flesh eaters a sinners diet"

(Balance pg. 31)

1. A spiritual definition for the word "flesh" is one's sinful tendencies.
2. The overall message here is to say that those who make a lifestyle out of sin are only focused on their own desires and not the desires of God. Therefore, they are full of themselves by way of being selfish in their sinful nature.

"They out here preaching

that's why you see all these sinners dying"

(Balance pg. 32)

1. "Death" here is being used in the spiritual sense. In John Chapter 3, Jesus tells the religious teacher Nicodemus that, "unless someone is born again, they cannot see the kingdom of God."

Defining "the kingdom of God" is a 2-fold meaning.

On one hand, it refers to Heaven, while on the other hand, it's the comprehensive rule and authority God has over someone's life.

In order for someone to submit to God's authority over their life, they would have to put to death their selfish, sinful desires and be reborn.

The reborn process is through baptism of both water and Spirit. It is through the Spirit, however, that believers are equipped with the spiritual power and boldness to go forth and carry out the assignments of the Kingdom.

2. So, the overall message here is saying that people who were once sinners are now submitting their lives over to God, dying to their own lifestyles, and preaching the transformative power of Jesus Christ to those who do not yet know.

You can't live until you die, bruh get it right....

You can't live until you die bruh, get a life"

(Balance pg. 32)

1. As stated in the above breakdown, in order for someone to submit to God's authority over their life, they would have to die to their selfish sinful desires.

   The lifestyles controlled by our sinful desires equate to spiritual death, which unfortunately in most cases, results in eternal separation from God, or hell.

   That is said because most of the time, the individual sees nothing wrong with the lifestyle they are living, thus making the idea of repentance or apologizing to God irrelevant.

In order to receive salvation and gain access into heaven, however, one must admit that they are flawed, while believing in Christ Jesus and His death, burial, and resurrection as the only source of rectification for our sins.

When this happens, new life begins for that individual; until that happens, the individual is considered as living a life outside of the will of God.

"I know some folks that when tested they gotta get a light"

(Balance pg. 32)

1. Meaning that when some folks are tested, they need a lighter to smoke a cigarette to calm their nerves.

"When Abraham got tested he had to get a knife"

(Balance pg. 32)

1. In Genesis Chapter 22, God tested Abraham to see if he really trusted, loved, and feared Him. He had Abraham take his only son, Isaac, up on a mountain, tie him up, and offer him as a burnt offering unto the Lord. Abraham did as he was told, and after tying up his son, he pulled out a knife and raised it to kill Isaac – only to be stopped by the angel of the Lord.

"will you let, God enter or fight

The inner god in you"

(Balance pg. 32)

1. "Inner god" refers to our spirit-man, who we were made in the image of God as.
2. Overall meaning, will we allow God to penetrate and transform our lives, or will we wrestle against His spirit that dwells within us and continue to live sinful lives.

"Appreciate your history and don't become a Tobey"

(Balance pg. 32)

1. Overall meaning, know who God has created you to be, and don't conform to who anyone else classifies you as.

"Spur of the moment went Ginobli"

(Balance pg. 32)

1. The play on words here is with "spur."
2. The term "spur of the moment" means "in the blink of an eye," or "at the last minute."
3. Manu Ginobli was a Spanish NBA player that played his full career with the San Antonio Spurs from 2002-2018.

"But honestly Ima need

for you all to stay in my lane

As spiritual speed bumps"

(Balance pg. 34)

1. Meaning, to be held accountable and not become self-righteous, I embrace critics for the benefit of slowing down my pride and strengthening my humility.

"Instead of looking like Christ

I'm looking like a religion"

(Balance pg. 34)

1. Meaning that my actions no longer reflected the heart of Christ, but rather the insensitivity of religion.

"a Warrior inside your oracle"

(Balance pg. 34)

1. The play on word here is "oracle."

2. In 1st Kings Chapter 6, Solomon was building the Lord's temple. It was in verse 16 that his construction began on the oracle, which was also called the most holy place.

3. Because of Jesus' death, resurrection, and ascension, believers now have direct access to God, and no longer have to rely on the high priest to take their prayers and requests through a veil into the most holy place. So, with me having direct access to God, I am to come boldly before Him as one of His warriors.

4. The arena of the NBA team The Golden State Warriors is called The Oracle.

"you've called me only to fight and not end up Saul on my knife"

(Balance pg. 35)

1. Saul was a king who paved a destructive path for himself based on his decisions and disobedience against the Lord. He ended up killing himself by falling on his own sword.

2. I've been called to fight for the gospel of Christ Jesus, and to do so by submitting myself to His will. Anything outside of that would essentially be me killing myself, such as Saul did.

"but I see....

Me killing myself was all a part of my Christ....

Sacrificing the body for better

part of the price

he paid..."

(Balance pg. 35)

1. "Me killing myself" means me dying to my own desires.
2. "Was all a part of my Christ," means Christ desired to have the Father remove the obligation of dying for the sins of the world, but instantly doubled-back by saying not His will, but that the Father's will might be done.
3. "Sacrificing the body for better," means Christ sacrificed His own body for the betterment of all humanity.

"My mirror is suffering because of it"

(My Obedience pg. 53)

1. I am hurting due to my own decisions.

"Asi Asi feelin so so...."

(My Obedience pg. 53)

1. "Asi Asi" in spanish means "so so."

"I don't wanna be Jonah in the whale...."

(My Obedience pg. 54)

1. Jonah was swallowed by a whale due to his disobedience to God's instructions.

"I need grace, I'm here at the well....."

(My Obedience pg. 54)

1. In John 4:6, it reads that Jesus was tired from His travels, so He sat down at Jacob's well.
2. The overall imagery is that I'm willing to position myself where Jesus is, because I'm seeking His grace.

"....Living water submerge me"

(My Obedience pg. 54)

1. It was in John 4:10 that Jesus told the Samaritan woman, "If you knew the gift of God, and who is saying to you, Give me a drink, you would ask him, and he would give you living water." He later goes on to say in verse 14, "But whoever drinks of the water that I will give him will never get thirsty again. In fact, the water I will give him will become a well of water springing up in him for eternal life." The living water mentioned here refers to Holy Spirit.
2. The overall meaning is me asking Holy Spirit to totally take me under His power.

"But I'm finessing your grace like a finger-roll"

(My Obedience pg. 56)

1. A "finger-roll" is a basketball term referring to a very smooth lay-up that rolls off of the shooter's fingertips.
2. The definition of finesse is extreme delicacy, or to use a synonym, smooth.

3. The overall meaning is that I was taking the grace that God had bestowed upon me and smoothly operated in a way of satisfying my own desires.

"My stomach in knots

a figure four"

(My Obedience pg. 56)

1. "My stomach in knots" had a double meaning. The first meaning is based off of the line prior to this where I say, "I'm sick of my sin and that's literal."

    Typically, when one is sick to his stomach, they use the term of their stomach being in knots. The second meaning has to do with a literal knot, which then transitions over into the definition of what a figure-four is. A figure-four is a wrestling move in which one wrestler tangles his opponent into a very tight and uncomfortable position.

"Be feeling like regurgitating throwing up my set"

(My Own Thorn pg. 62)

1. Refer to page 144 ("throwing up E-Town wit a cup full of liquor").

"Living in circles....only Jehovah knows my reps"

(My Own Thorn pg. 63)

1. A rep is a shortened way of saying repetition. A repetition is the act of repeating something over and over.
2. The overall meaning here is only God knew how many times I kept ending up back at the same place in life due to my decisions.

"I'm weaker than 7 days"

(Be Your Wind pg. 63)

1. The play on words here is "weak."
2. On one hand, I'm calling myself weak, while on the other hand, using weak as week in reference to 7 days.

"Them same ones writing providing you skewed views

Could be them same ones beside you providing a new noose"

(Be Your Wind pg. 64)

1. A skewed view is one that is misleading, unfair, distorted, or biased.
2. The overall message here is that the people providing you misleading information could also equate to one handing you a rope to hang yourself with.
3. Not all provisions are worth your time.

"You seen me living so aimlessly

Yet

You targeted me with deliverance"

(Be Your Wind pg. 72)

1. To live aimlessly means to live in a way of having no sense of direction; however, God made it His mission to pin-point, select, and bless me with a life better than the one I had prior to Him.

"only L I know is Lord"

(Be Your Wind pg. 73)

1. Taking a "L" is a slang term in the competitive world meaning to take a "loss."
2. Here, I'm basically saying that I don't know of any losses; instead, I only know the Lord.

"Never ever will you catch me on the bench

I just wanna be your....wind"

(Be Your Wind pg. 74)

1. The play on words here is "wind," which I'm using as "win."
2. The overall meaning is that I will not remain on the sideline for God, but rather, He will see my efforts in His will being done on earth.

"Duckin shots from the opps"

(Conviction pg. 78)

1. This is a slang term meaning "to evade gunfire from the rivals."

"I was good inside the mud"

(Conviction pg. 79)

1. "Mud" is a slang term symbolizing "the streets," or "from nothing."
2. The overall meaning here is how I exuded that I didn't need His help because I felt as though I was good when I was living the life I lived prior to His embrace.

"Timbs"

(Conviction pg. 79)

1. "Timbs" are short for the brand of boots called Timberlands.

"I had a daughter by my sin"

(Conviction pg. 79)

1. The overall meaning here is that I had a daughter outside of marriage and within my lifestyle of fornication.

"You said I must die to myself you knew I'd be my weapon"

(Conviction pg. 79)

1. The overall meaning here was me referring to how God knew that in order for me to return back into His arms, it would be me sacrificing my own desires to live according to His will for my life.

"You said the wages of sin is death

so your crucifixion

Was payment for another

cuz you said you held no blemish"

(Conviction pg. 80)

1. "The wages of sin is death," is a portion of scripture referenced in Romans 6:23, meaning that the payment for disobeying God's divine instruction is separation from Him.
2. The overall meaning here is me saying that since God made no mistakes, His reason for being crucified had to be spiritually predicated on what those around Him did.

"You said yo temple would be broken

in 3 days re-risen

And you said our bodies are a temple

we must see Your vision"

(Conviction pg. 80)

1. When Jesus spoke of a temple in John 2:19, He was referring to His actual body; the same way He was referring to our individual bodies when He mentioned the temple in 1 Corinthians 3:16.

"itchin for that bump"

(Conviction pg. 81)

1. Is a slang term meaning "feening for another hit of a drug," typically drugs that are injected, such as crack or heroin.

"He suppose to be our answer

when it don't add up to sum"

(Conviction pg. 81)

1. The play on word here is "sum," which I'm also using as "some."
2. The mathematical definition of the word "sum" means total or answer.
3. Overall meaning here is that God is supposed to be our final answer in life, whether it makes sense to others or not.

"And as long as the body continues to waver

we will all be dim as one"

(Conviction pg. 81)

1. "The body" means followers of Christ as a whole.
2. The overall meaning here is that as long as the followers of Jesus Christ continue to be hesitant in their approach to boldly represent Christ, then their influence on earth will have very little effect.

"I'm just praying He would place us back in the mud

rain down His saliva

Smear it over our eyes

So that we can see Him proper"

(Conviction pg. 81)

1. This entire passage is referring to the healing of the blind man that took place in John Chapter 9 where Jesus spat on the ground and made mud. Jesus took the mud and smeared it on a man's eyes who was born blind. He then had the man go and wash in a river which restored his vision.

2. The overall meaning here derives from a place of me saying that I wish God would take the drastic measure of removing His grace from us by placing us back in the crappy lifestyles we were in.

   Take something as vile and disgusting as spit, while making it known to us what's being done.

Use the disgusting thing to correct our lifestyles once more so that we can clearly see His restorative power and abilities in using anything to bring forth His will on earth.

All being done before us so we will have no room to take any of His credit or touch any of His glory.

"eternal separation"

(Conviction pg. 81)

1. "Eternal Separation" is the spiritual definition for "hell."

"I was Jacob and Jonah wrestling God from within"

(His Love pg. 87)

1. In Genesis 32:24, Jacob literally wrestled an angel of the Lord. His battle was more of a spiritual battle, however, because it was an extreme measure of his faith.

Jonah's battle, on the other hand, was a different story.

The Lord told Jonah to go and preach repentance to the city of Nineveh, but instead, Jonah fled to Tarshish.

Jonah battled with obeying the Lord, because he didn't feel that the people of Nineveh were deserving of the Lord's mercy.

2. Overall meaning, my biggest battle with God was in my faith, which tainted my obedience.

"Pandora's box I opened but by His grace I survived"

(His Love pg. 87)

1. "Pandora's Box" can be defined as a prolific source of troubles.
2. The overall meaning here is that I made the decision to indulge in a sin that could've led to dire consequences, but God's grace allowed me to recognize and replace those desires.

"The sheep know the voice of their shepherd"

(His Love pg. 88)

1. In John Chapter 10, Jesus compares sheep to His followers, and Himself to the "Good Shepherd." He explains how in the same way sheep know the voice of the shepherd and adheres to their demands, His followers also know His voice and follow His commandments.

"Enabling those with ears to hear to not be spiritually numb"

(His Love pg. 88)

1. Jesus used this phrase several times to differentiate between those who understood His spiritual terminologies and those who didn't.

   In John Chapter 14, Jesus explained to His disciples the significance of Holy Spirit, who was to come to those who believed.

In John 14:26, He explained how "Holy Spirit would teach them all things to bring to remembrance all of His teachings." For those with Holy Spirit, they would not only feel God's presence, but also His divine guidance as He speaks to their spirit.

"Agape is His cologne heaven scent for our direction"

(His Love pg. 90)

1. The definition for agape is "God's heavenly love."
2. The play on words here is "heaven scent," which is also compared to "heaven sent."
3. Christ was heaven sent for our direction back to the Father, while God's love (agape) can be seen as His very essence, or, His heavenly scent.

"The word of God is sharp fileting the adversary"

(Hallelujah pg. 97)

1. Hebrews 4:12 says, "For the word of God is living and active. Sharper than any double-edged sword, it pierces even to dividing soul and spirit, joints and marrow. It judges the thoughts and intentions of the heart."

"I was made from dirt so I get it out the mud"

(Hallelujah pg. 97)

1. Genesis 2:7 explains how God took dust from the ground and formed man's body.
2. "Mud" is a slang term symbolizing "the streets" or "from nothing."

"You don't want know problems get calculatored"

(Hallelujah pg. 97)

1. The purpose of a calculator is to solve a mathematical problem.

"I'm no Patty Mayo get out my way Doug"

(Hallelujah pg. 97)

1. Patty Mayo was a character on the cartoon series titled "Doug."

"Imago Dei"

(Hallelujah pg. 97)

1. "Imago Dei" means image of God in Latin.

"Yahweh"

(Hallelujah pg. 97)

1. "Yahweh" is the name of God.

"living waters flowing from our guts"

(Hallelujah pg. 97)

1. John 7:38 Jesus speaks of living waters flowing from within those who believe in Him.

   The living water He is referring to is Holy Spirit.

This lyric is me identifying myself as a believer who is filled with Holy Spirit.

"But came...up...

like Weezy

And George"

(Hallelujah pg. 99)

1. Weezy and George were characters from the famous 1975 sitcom, "The Jeffersons;" the opening theme song to the show was entitled "Movin' On Up."

"See I remember being all up in the world like, oxygen and then my God, pulled me out, like a splinter"

(God's Got Me pg. 102)

1. "Being in the world," references the old life I once lived, until God transformed my life, OR "pulled me out" of that lifestyle

"in Him, I could fall, like November"

(God's Got Me pg. 102)

1. November is a month that lies in the "fall" season.
2. In Jesus I could "fall;" meaning, in Him I can cast all of my cares and rest without worry.

"Now da boy a son, of a king, call me Simba"

(God's Got Me pg. 103)

1. This line is referring to "The Lion King," where Simba was the son of Mufasa who was king; however, the king I'm referring to is Jesus Christ.

"The Godhead 3 in 1 Father Spirit and Son

Is like ice water steam all 3 are 1"

(God's Got Me pg. 105)

1. "The Godhead" refers to God's triune nature; meaning, Him being God the Father, God the Son, and God the Holy Spirit.

The analogy used to describe this was ice, water, and steam.

All 3 are technically water, although they take on different forms and functions.

I'd like to correct this example, however, by stating that the ice, water, and steam analogy is not the best description of The Godhead.

When water is frozen, it's no longer water but ice. When ice is melted, it's no longer ice but water. When water is boiled, what rises is no longer water but steam. The individual identities change based upon their conditions. That's not the same with God.

He does not have to stop being God the Father in order to be God the Son or Holy Spirit. God is one in nature, and at the same time, 3 co-equal persons. (*I grew to understand this months after the release of this song. I pray this clears up any confusion on the matter.*)

"In timbos"

(All By Myself pg. 111)

1. "Timbos" is a nickname for the brand of boots called "Timberlands."

"you take more L's than Snoop do"

(All By Myself pg. 111)

1. For one to "take a L" is slang meaning they've taken a loss.
2. A "L" is also a slang term for a rolled up blunt of weed.
3. Snoop being mentioned here is referring to the famous rapper Snoop Dogg who is known for smoking weed.

"We all W's wit it like Snoop dude"

(All By Myself pg. 111)

1. The opposite of taking a "L", which is a loss, would be to take a "W", which is a win.
2. Snoop Dogg is also known for throwing up W's with his fingers, representing "West Side," since he is from California.

185

"we don't spit Crip no bluetooth"

(All By Myself pg. 111)

1. "Spit" is slang for rap.
2. Crip is a gang which is known for wearing the color blue.
3. Bluetooth is a play on me saying "spit," which typically involves teeth, or the lack there-of, and blue which is the color Crips wear.

"Only rep the blood but no suwoop"

(All By Myself pg. 111)

1. "The blood" has two meanings. One meaning is the blood of Jesus, and the other is another well known gang called The Bloods.
2. "SuWoop" is a common greeting amongst The Blood gang members.

"give em straight Word like doop doop"

(All By Myself pg. 111)

1. "Doop Doop" symbolizes the sound of an automatic high-powered rifle.

"My pedigree is on woof woof"

(All By Myself pg. 111)

1. Woof woof emphasizes the bark of a big dog.
2. The definition of pedigree here is a distinguished lineage.

"cuz my God reigns till the roof loose"

(All By Myself pg. 111)

1. The entendre here is in the word reign and rain.
2. Reign means to have dominating power or influence.
3. The overall meaning here is that God will be dominate on His throne for a very long time.

"Straight up the gut like I'm seven Rays"

(All By Myself pg. 113)

1. The Ray being mentioned here is the NFL Hall Of Fame Player, Ray Lewis, who played middle linebacker for the Baltimore Ravens.

   Ray did some of the most damage when he would come straight up the middle and either sack the quarterback, or meet the running back head on for a powerful tackle.

"with an unleavened taste"

(All By Myself pg. 113)

1. The overall meaning here is to have a taste that includes nothing extra that would dilute it or distort it from being 100% pure.

"A-Town stumping on the devil's face"

(All By Myself pg. 113)

1. The "A-Town" stomp was a dance move created in the early 2000's by rappers from Atlanta.

"mortal kombat but I'm Luke Cage

..... double edged with 2 blades

Baraka like in the Dark Knight I am walking light go from Lui Kang into Bruce Wayne you'll get saufleed"

(All By Myself pg. 113)

1. Luke Cage was a fictional character from Marvel comic books who was a black man.
2. Mortal Kombat is an American series of video games which also became movies.
3. Baraka was a fictional character from Mortal Kombat who had a long double-edged blade as each hand.
4. The entendre here is the double-edged blade, because Hebrews 4:12 states how the word of God is sharper than any two-edged sword.

5. Dark Knight is a 2008 superhero movie based off Dc Comics superhero Batman.
6. Lui Kang is a fictional character off of Mortal Kombat, whose signature move was to shoot fire from his hands at his opponents, while Bruce Wayne was the fictitious name of Batman.
7. The entendre here is me saying "dark knight," and then identifying myself as "walking light," based on Matthew 5:14, which says that believers are the light of the world.

"sins payment is your doomsday"

(All By Myself pg. 113)

1. Romans 6:23 says that the wages of sin is death.

"A young Jonah I almost sank the boat"

(G.o.E pt.4 pg. 116)

1. In the book of Jonah, it tells us how in the midst of his disobedience to God, he boarded a ship that would take him opposite of where God told him to go.

While on the ship, God caused a storm to beat against the ship and almost break it apart.

2. The overall meaning here is due to my blatant disregard for God's instruction over my life, I almost destroyed everything and everyone around me.

"Gary Payton how I plays Him close"

(G.o.E pt.4 pg. 116)

1. NBA superstar Gary Payton was most known for his tenacious defense, which is why his nickname was "the glove."

"It's Christ Jesus the Lamb...

Yeshua when I thank the g.o.a.t"

(G.o.E pt.4 pg. 116)

1. The significance of a lamb in the scriptures is that they were the primary animal used as offerings of sacrifice.

The killing of a lamb without blemish would cover the sin of the trespasser.

This ritual, however, would have to be done for every transgression that took place.

That was until Christ Jesus sacrificed Himself for the sins of all humanity, once and for all.

Yeshua, or Jesus, was then called the Lamb, due to Him being the sacrifice that had no blemish.

2. G.O.A.T is an acronym for "greatest of all time."

3. The play on words here is with lamb and goat, in which people often confuse the two; however, I am identifying Christ as the Lamb, and stating that He is the greatest of all time.

"Set fire to any track so His name I toast call it communion"

(G.o.E pt.4 pg. 116)

1. To "set fire to a track" means to do an incredibly great job at rapping a song.

2. Toast is bread that is browned by heat.

3. In Luke 22:19, Jesus took bread, gave thanks to God for it, broke it, gave it to His disciples, told them that it was His body, and to eat in remembrance of Him. Along with Jesus also doing this with wine, the overall occasion was called "communion."

"We on one accord no Ford Fusion"

(G.o.E pt.4 pg. 116)

1. To be on one accord refers to the body of Christ being unified.
2. "Accord" here is also being referenced to the car Honda Accord, which is not a Ford Fusion.

"I'm built Lord tough for this thang no joke"

(G.o.E pt.4 pg. 116)

1. The slogan for Ford vehicles is that they are "Built Ford Tough." While still playing off the Ford Fusion line, I am saying that I am built Lord tough, for my Christian walk.

"Fugazi"

(G.o.E pt.4 pg. 117)

1. Fugazi means fake or unauthentic.

"I'd rather after a show you go repent instead of pay me

I know the industry say that don't make cents"

(G.o.E pt.4 pg. 117)

1. The play on words here is cents, because I am using it with the idea of payment, while at the same time, my decision not making "sense" to the industry.

"I veered off bag chasing in that clout game"

(G.o.E pt.4 pg. 117)

1. "Bag chasing" basically means to intentionally seek after money, while "clout" means to be famous while having influence.

2. The overall meaning here is that I began to care less about bringing people closer to Christ, and more about making myself known throughout the industry and making money.

"Money lookin Kevin Hart funny"

(G.o.E pt.4 pg. 117)

1. Kevin Hart is an American comedian.
2. For ones "money to look funny," basically means that the amount of money they have is below their liking or expectations.

"Tryna force out brainstorms within a drought mane"

(G.o.E pt.4 pg. 117)

1. The overall meaning here is me saying that I was trying to make music while being uninspired.

"I was lost in the sauce"

(G.o.E pt.4 pg. 117)

1. To be "lost in the sauce" means to have something good going your way, and then to start taking unnecessary risks or become out of touch with reality.

"Aiming for God's heart and completely missing the mark

......9:24 my unbelief is an of-course"

(G.o.E pt.4 pg. 117)

1. The play on words here is the word "mark."
2. To "miss the mark" basically means to come up short.
3. Mark 9:24 is where a father is having a conversation with Jesus and explains to Him that he does believe but he just needs help with his unbelief.

"Picture me, on the boat with Jesus thinking of jumping off

when the waves got rocky and suddenly came the storm"

(G.o.E pt.4 pg. 117)

1. In Mark 4:38, Jesus and His disciples were on a boat when a bad storm arose. Jesus was asleep during the storm while His disciples were panicking. In this line, I place myself in the boat as one of Jesus' disciples, while referring back to my own unbelief.

"kill my flesh and then hand chalk to you"

(G.o.E pt.4 pg. 118)

1. The overall meaning here is not only am I killing my old desires and unholy ways, but I am passing along the tools and way of thinking for you to do the same in your life.

"Sorta like me in my mirror examining what you hide"

(G.o.E pt.4 pg. 118)

1. The overall meaning here is that the same way Jesus' disciples walked alongside and saw Him perform miracles and were still confused as to who He was – is the same as me looking at myself in the mirror, yet seeing another persons' flaws. They were not able to see the truth for themselves due to their lack of spiritual vision.

"I'm 8 ball corner pocket

but I'm coming off the reel with every line I fish"

(G.o.E pt.4 pg. 119)

1. For one to call "8 ball corner pocket," typically means that they are on their final shot in a game of billiards.
2. "Reel" is a triple entendre, because I'm speaking of the reel on a pool table, a fishing reel, and also about the fact that I'm not lying; as in I'm coming off the real.

3. The overall meaning here is that even at my last shot, I'm going to be real and authentic in my approach when telling others about the gospel of Jesus Christ.

"I've changed no lie I don't do this for the fame nor vine"

(G.o.E pt.4 pg. 119)

1. The term "do it for the vine" came from viners doing crazy things and uploading it onto the Vine app.
2. The overall meaning here is I'm a different person who is focused on doing right by God and for God, and not for money or popularity.

"No chip on my shoulder I don't want no Frito Lays"

(G.o.E pt.4 pg. 119)

1. For one to have a "chip on his shoulder," means that he is arrogant and prideful.
2. I'm playing on the word "chip" here to basically say that I don't want anything to do with my prideful ways.

"They sleepin on Christ, iont entertain those lies"

(G.o.E pt.4 pg. 119)

1. One is usually "lying" down while asleep.

2. To "sleep on someone" means to underestimate them, or to not take them seriously.

3. I'm playing on the word "lies," while basically saying that I don't entertain the criticism from skeptics when it comes to Jesus Christ, because most of them are lying.

"My bets on Yeshua the rest, I just pay no mind"

(G.o.E pt.4 pg. 120)

The play on words here are with "bets" and "pay no mind."

The overall meaning here is that my full trust is in Jesus Christ.

Contact Jerrell Golden, Sr. via the information below:

Website: Jerrell-golden.online
Email: transparencythebook@gmail.com
Facebook: Transparency TheBook
Instagram: @transparency_thebook
TikTok: @transparency_thebook

Made in the USA
Middletown, DE
01 May 2023

29796170R00116